THE CAMBRIDGE BIBLE COMMENTARY

NEW ENGLISH BIBLE

GENERAL EDITORS

P. R. ACKROYD, A. R. C. LEANEY, J. W. PACKER

THE REVELATION
OF JOHN

THE REVELATION OF
JOHN

COMMENTARY BY

T. F. GLASSON

Lecturer in New Testament Studies
New College, London

CAMBRIDGE
AT THE UNIVERSITY PRESS
1965

PUBLISHED BY
THE SYNDICS OF THE CAMBRIDGE UNIVERSITY PRESS

Bentley House, 200 Euston Road, London, N.W. 1
American Branch: 32 East 57th Street, New York 22, N.Y.
West African Office: P.O. Box 33, Ibadan, Nigeria

©

CAMBRIDGE UNIVERSITY PRESS

1965

TO
MILLIE AND ERNEST

GENERAL EDITORS' PREFACE

The aim of this series is to provide the text of the New English Bible closely linked to a commentary in which the results of modern scholarship are made available to the general reader. Teachers and young people preparing for such examinations as the General Certificate of Education at Ordinary or Advanced Level in Britain, and similar qualifications elsewhere have been especially kept in mind. The commentators have been asked to assume no specialized theological knowledge, and no knowledge of Greek and Hebrew. Bare references to other literature and multiple references to other parts of the Bible have been avoided. Actual quotations have been given as often as possible.

Within these quite severe limits each commentator will attempt to set out the main findings of recent New Testament scholarship, and to describe the historical background to the text. The main theological content of the New Testament will also be critically discussed.

Much attention has been given to the form of the volumes. The aim is to produce books each of which will be read consecutively from first to last page. The introductory material leads naturally into the text, which itself leads into the alternating sections of commentary. By this means it is hoped that each book will be easily read and remain in the mind as a unity.

The series will be prefaced by a volume—*Understanding the New Testament*—which will outline the larger historical background, say something about the growth and transmission of the text, and answer the question 'Why should we study the New Testament?' Another volume—*The New Testament Illustrated*—will contain maps, diagrams and photographs.

P. R. A.
A. R. C. L.
J. W. P.

EDITOR'S PREFACE

I am indebted to the editors for their careful scrutiny of my notes, and I have taken advantage of a large number of suggestions they have made towards clarifying the meaning. I am also grateful to the editorial staff and craftsmen of the Cambridge University Press for their watchfulness and skill, and to my wife for valuable help with the index.

T. F. G.

CONTENTS

LIST OF ROMAN EMPERORS

The following list of Roman emperors will be found useful for reference:

Augustus	27 B.C. to A.D. 14
Tiberius	A.D. 14 to 37
Caligula	A.D. 37 to 41
Claudius	A.D. 41 to 54
Nero	A.D. 54 to 68
Galba	A.D. 68 to 69
Otho	A.D. 69
Vitellius	A.D. 69
Vespasian	A.D. 69 to 79
Titus	A.D. 79 to 81
Domitian	A.D. 81 to 96

0   10 20 30 40 50 miles

·········· Provincial boundary

THE PROVINCE OF ASIA (WESTERN PART)

THE REVELATION
OF JOHN

✻ ✻ ✻ ✻ ✻ ✻ ✻ ✻ ✻ ✻ ✻ ✻ ✻ ✻

The Revelation of John is the only book of its kind in the
New Testament. Elsewhere we have narrative (the Gospels
and Acts) and letters (Romans to Jude). But this book presents a different type of writing. The Greek title is *apokalupsis*,
which produces the English word apocalypse, and the book
of Revelation is sometimes known as the Apocalypse.

WHAT IS AN APOCALYPSE?

The word means an uncovering, an unveiling, either (*a*) of
future events, or (*b*) of the unseen realms of heaven and hell.
There are many apocalypses in existence; one of the best
known is the book of Daniel, the apocalyptic part being
found mainly in chapters 7–12. Outside the Bible there are such
books as 2 Esdras (in the Apocrypha), 2 Baruch and Enoch.

Prophetic and apocalyptic writings are closely related and
cannot be entirely separated; they overlap and one class runs
over into the other. But broadly speaking they represent
different tendencies and emphases. The difference can be
better felt than defined; when we read the book of Enoch we
feel that we are in a somewhat different world from that of
Amos and Isaiah. The following points draw out some of the
contrasts, at the risk of some simplification; in a fuller statement
all kinds of qualifications would need to be made.

(1) A prophecy was usually *spoken*, though it may be pre-
served to us in a written form. Such men as Isaiah, Jeremiah
and Amos spoke their messages publicly. The apocalypses on

I

the contrary were, as a rule, *written* products from the start. One can hardly imagine chapters of Enoch or Revelation being delivered in the open air. They are more artificial and less spontaneous than prophetic utterances.

(2) Prophecy is usually given in straightforward terms, but the apocalypses frequently adopted what we may call 'cartoon' language. We are accustomed to newspaper cartoons in which Russia is represented by a bear, England by a lion, China by a dragon. This will help us to understand the language of these books. An apocalypse is usually something of a riddle, and the weird pictures may be interpreted in different ways. Part of the reason for this is that it would be dangerous to speak of a ruler or a nation by name. But cryptic symbols would avoid such a risk.

(3) Apocalypses were usually written at a time of crisis and danger. One of their purposes was to strengthen the believer at a time of persecution and to encourage him to stand firm. This is true of the book of Daniel which appeared in the second century B.C., when the Jews were fiercely persecuted for their faith. Although apocalypses spring from profound faith and burning conviction, the writers generally despair of the present and pin all their hopes on the future. They look for some great divine intervention in the near future, often on a world-wide scale, to put an end to an intolerable situation. It is true that the prophets also looked for divine action in the future; but there was a difference. The prophets appealed to men to change their attitude in order that by their repentance the threatened doom might be withdrawn (cf. Jonah 3: 10, 'And God saw their works, that they turned from their evil way; and God repented of the evil, which he said he would do unto them; and he did it not'). But with the apocalyptists there was a kind of *fatalism*. The future was fixed and ordered according to a divine calendar of events; this is 'what must shortly happen' (Rev. 1: 1) and no human action can alter it.

(4) Many apocalypses were written under assumed names.

No one believes that Enoch and Elijah actually wrote the books which pass under their names. This 'pseudonymity', as we call it, is not invariable but it applies to a large number of these books. It does not hold true, in the main, of the great prophets of the Bible.

In the case of the book of Revelation, points (1), (2) and (3) apply; but as far as (4) is concerned, there is no reason to believe that it was written under an assumed name. The writer tells us his name was John (1: 1, 4, 9) and we have no grounds for doubting this.

WHO WAS JOHN?

Long tradition has ascribed five writings of the New Testament to the Apostle John, the son of Zebedee: the Fourth Gospel, the three Johannine epistles, and the book of Revelation. But there are grave difficulties in this view. While the Gospel and the epistles are similar in style to each other, the Revelation is very different and has a type of Greek which is unique; it is full of grammatical irregularities though the writer uses it with powerful effect. Again, the thought of the writer of Revelation—his hopes, his view of Christianity—provides a marked contrast with the thought of the Gospel and the epistles. As long ago as the third century, a bishop of Alexandria named Dionysius saw that it was almost impossible to ascribe all the five works to a single writer. He suggested that the Gospel and epistles were written by the Apostle, and Revelation by another John.

A little later Eusebius, bishop of Caesarea, in his famous *History of the Church* quoted a passage from a writer of the early second century named Papias, which seemed (though this is far from certain) to distinguish two Johns: the Apostle John and John the Elder. Eusebius thought this might provide a solution for the problem; the book of Revelation (which he did not like) could be ascribed to John the Elder, and the other Johannine writings to the Apostle.

It is impossible to mention all the theories about the authorship of the Johannine writings which have been put forward. Some authorities have pointed to the fact that the sons of Zebedee, James and John, were called by Jesus 'sons of thunder' and such a nickname could well be applied to the author of Revelation. All we can say with fair certainty is that the book was written by a Christian named John, who was for a time banished to the island of Patmos. He had a connexion of some kind with the seven churches of Asia Minor to which he writes; but he was not necessarily a church leader. He was a man of visionary and prophetic gifts who felt led to write this book as a message from God to the churches. The fact that he calls himself John without any title or description beyond the words in 1: 9 suggests that he was not John the son of Zebedee; and there are other reasons which suggest that he was not the Apostle. He writes as 'I, John, your brother, who share with you in the suffering and the sovereignty and the endurance which is ours in Jesus'. From the contents of the book we may gather with some certainty that he was a Jewish Christian.

Patmos was used as a place of exile to which prisoners could be sent, and the words of the opening chapter suggest that John had been banished there as a punishment for his Christian allegiance and witness. The island lies in the Aegean Sea, between Turkey and Greece. It is about 30 miles from the mainland which in those days was known as the Roman province of Asia, the western portion of what we sometimes call Asia Minor. Patmos is almost due west of Miletus, the coastal town where Paul met the Ephesian elders (Acts 20: 15–17). The seven churches to which John wrote letters (chs. 2–3) were all situated in Asia. (See map on p. xi.)

HOW WAS THE BOOK RECEIVED BY THE CHURCH?

If the book had been known from the beginning to be the work of an Apostle, it would be difficult to understand the slowness with which it gained acceptance throughout the

4

Christian world. One reason for the opposition of certain authorities in early centuries was the teaching of Rev. 20 concerning the Millennium; it is stated there that when Jesus returns to the earth he will reign for a thousand years with the resurrected martyrs. This doctrine, known as millenarianism, was believed literally by certain early Christian writers, such as Justin Martyr and Irenaeus. It flourished mainly in Asia Minor, the very area from which the book of Revelation emerged. It is inconsistent with the main stream of Christian thought, which has preferred to emphasize the fact that Jesus has already begun his reign. The frequency with which Ps. 110 is quoted in the New Testament shows that this is a basic conviction of the faith. This is the psalm which begins, 'The Lord saith unto my lord, Sit thou at my right hand...'.

It was Augustine, the bishop of Hippo (354–430), who gave the final blow to millenarianism; he said that the Millennium is not a literal period of time or a visible reign. The Millennium in Rev. 20, he said, begins with the binding of Satan (20: 2–3) and this took place at Christ's first coming; it was then that Satan was bound, for Jesus himself in Mark 3: 27 spoke of his work in terms of binding the strong man, that is, the devil. This explanation of Augustine, while not an accurate interpretation of Rev. 20, brought John's conception of the reign of Christ into line with the rest of the New Testament. Augustine's contemporary Jerome included Revelation in the Vulgate, his Latin translation of the Bible; and through the predominant influence of Augustine and Jerome, further resistance to the book was difficult in the west.

The eastern communities, however, in some areas hesitated for centuries. Revelation was not at first included among the Scriptures used at Antioch. And when the New Testament was translated into Syriac, it did not contain this book. Even as late as the eleventh century its position as scripture was not undisputed. A few centuries after this, when the Reformation period began, its place was again in jeopardy in the west. Luther at first did not accept it as a book of scripture, and he placed it with a few other New Testament writings in an appendix to the Bible devoted to works of inferior authority. Calvin, who wrote commentaries on most books of the Bible, missed out the book of Revelation, evidently sharing Luther's feelings. Zwingli, the Swiss Reformer, said, 'It is not a book of the Bible'.

In spite of all this one cannot help feeling that the book of Revelation provides a climax for the Scriptures. Its skilful weaving together of strands taken from many parts of the Old Testament makes it a kind of triumphant finale to the Bible; it reminds us of a composer gathering up the themes of his symphony in a closing burst of glorious music. Some of its teaching strikes us as unchristian: pictures of horses wading in deep pools of pagan blood (14: 20), the apparent gloating over the appalling sufferings and judgements which await the enemies of the Church, torment day and night for ever (20: 10)—these things are hard to reconcile with the God and Father of our Lord Jesus Christ. But it must be remembered that this writing emerged from a period of bitter persecution and critical danger for the whole Christian cause in the world. It can only be understood in the light of its historical background, and to this we now turn.

THE BACKGROUND IN HISTORY

The 'Babylon' of the book stands for the persecuting Roman empire. Babylon is also used to indicate Rome in 1 Pet. 5: 13. The heavenly city of God is contrasted with Babylon; and after the latter has finally gone up in flames, the new Jerusalem comes down out of heaven from God. This is one instance of several contrasting pairs; thus we have the beast and the Lamb; the great whore and the Lamb's bride; the dragon or Satan standing over against God himself. Some of these parallels are worked out in detail; thus the very phrase concerning the Lamb, 'with the marks of slaughter upon him', is used also of the beast. We shall see the meaning of these phrases when we come to them. Our point at the moment is that the great enemy of the cause of God in the world is Babylon, standing for the persecuting Roman empire and demanding worship for its emperor.

Two Roman emperors are of special importance in understanding the book (for a list of Roman emperors see p. x):

(1) *Nero* (*54–68*), the first great persecutor of the Church, who killed Paul and probably Peter too. He murdered his own mother and kicked his wife so severely that she died. At the time of the great fire of Rome in A.D. 64, a rumour started that Nero himself was responsible for the blaze. So he had to find a scapegoat, and blamed the Christians of Rome. As Tacitus (*c.* 54–120), the famous Roman historian put it, 'So in order to drown the rumour, Nero shifted the guilt on persons known to the people as Christians, and punished them with exquisite tortures' (*Annals* 15: 44). This is the first mention of Christians by a Roman historian. Tacitus refers to the fact that Christ had been sentenced by Pontius Pilate; and he goes on to describe Nero's treatment of the Christians; some were crucified, others were mauled by dogs, others were set on fire and burnt after twilight by way of nightly illuminations in Nero's own gardens. Even the people of Rome, he says, at last began to feel pity for the Christians.

It was not long after this that the dissatisfaction with Nero's rule was so strong that he was forced to commit suicide. Strange to say, a belief soon arose that he was not really dead but was in hiding in the east and would later be returning at the head of the Parthian army to destroy Rome. Later several pretenders appeared, claiming to be Nero. Another form of the belief was that Nero was actually dead but would come to life again.

Now, the Jews had long believed that some great figure of evil would arise at the end of the age as the great enemy of God. Some of them came to think that Nero when he returned would be this 'man of sin'. Here is a quotation from a Jewish writing in which this belief is expressed:

'In the time of the end, and the last days of the moon, there shall be a mad, world-wide war, treacherous and guileful. And from the ends of the earth shall come the man who slew his mother, a fugitive, pondering piercing counsels in his mind, who shall subdue all the earth...and the city which caused him to fall, he shall capture at a blow.' (H. N. Bate's trans.)

This comes from a work known as the Sibylline Oracles, book 5: 361–8; 'the man who slew his mother' is clearly Nero. Several other examples could be given. But the point at the moment is that if Jews adopted this widespread belief about the return of Nero, it is not surprising that the same belief was adopted by the Christians. This is what we find in the book of Revelation. Nero is the beast's head, smitten unto death and yet his death-stroke was healed (13: 3). Again in chapter 17 mention is made of 'the beast that once was alive and is alive no longer', and yet comes back to reign again (17: 11). See also 11: 7, 'the beast that comes up from the abyss'.

This belief lingered for centuries. Even Augustine, 300 years later, mentions that some people thought that Nero would rise again and be the Antichrist, and that others thought he was not really dead but was still alive at the same age and vigour at which he was slain, until the time should come for him to return to his kingdom. (We may recall that long after the death of the German emperor Frederick Barbarossa he was said to be asleep in a cave. In the present century, after Hitler's suicide some believed or feared he was still alive and in hiding.)

(2) *Domitian (81–96)*. It is generally thought that Revelation was completed in Domitian's reign; this tradition goes back to Irenaeus (end of second century). Domitian extended persecution of the Church to a much wider area, Nero's activities being confined to Rome itself. Now there was 'a

succession of sharp, sudden partial assaults, striking down one here and one there from malice or jealousy or caprice, and harassing the Church with an agony of suspense'. There were traces of insanity about him; the poet Juvenal said that to talk with Domitian about the weather was to risk your life. He took much more seriously than his predecessors the issue of emperor-worship. He ordered all official proclamations to begin with formulae recognizing his deity. ('Our lord and god orders this to be done'). The aim was to consolidate the empire. To refuse to worship the emperor was treason.

Over a century earlier a temple for the worship of Rome and Augustus had been erected at Pergamum. It was the first of its kind in the province of Asia and this may help to explain Rev. 2: 13 where Pergamum is described as 'the home of Satan'; the same verse refers to Antipas who was martyred there. Another of these shrines was at Smyrna, and at the time of Domitian it was apparently the main centre of the cult in this area. The church of Smyrna must have had a specially hard ordeal and in the light of this we can appreciate the message to them in Rev. 2: 8–11. Incidentally, the 'dignitaries of the province' (Greek: *Asiarchs*) mentioned in Acts 19: 31 were the priests of emperor-worship. It is curious that there they are found befriending Paul at Ephesus. At that time the issue had not become acute and no pressure was put upon the Christians to share in this cult.

Emperor-worship, so important for our understanding of this book, is not merely a matter of ancient history. The whole question of the relation of the Church to the State is tied up with it. Again and again, Christians have had to resist claims made by human rulers which usurped the prerogatives of God. In the present century, the Christians of Japan and Germany have had to ask themselves if in responding to the increasing demands of the State rulers they were compromising their loyalty to Christ.

WHAT IS THE BOOK'S MEANING?

It is against this background of emperor-worship and persecution that the book can best be understood. The writer says
he is speaking of 'what must shortly happen' (1: 1); and we
must frankly admit that it did not happen. The various events
and woes outlined did not develop in the way John expected.
Nevertheless, the essential message of the book still stands.
It shows the invincible faith of the Christians at a crisis when
annihilation threatened them. The hymn verse adapted from
J. R. Lowell's lines expresses one of its main messages:

> Though the cause of evil prosper,
> Yet 'tis truth alone is strong;
> Though her portion be the scaffold,
> And upon the throne be wrong—
> Yet that scaffold sways the future,
> And, behind the dim unknown,
> Standeth God within the shadow,
> Keeping watch above His own.

When the connexion between Revelation and the events of
the first century was lost sight of, and the time for immediate
fulfilment of the prophecies had passed, the book came to be
regarded as a veiled account of the history of the world, from
the time of Christ to the end of history. It is curious to note
that whenever men look at Revelation in this way, they always
believe they themselves are living in the last time; they are
always in the period of chapters 17–18 or thereabouts.
Attempts to identify the beast, the figure of evil so prominent
in the book (sometimes called Antichrist), vary in this way
according to historical circumstances. Muhammad, the
Pope, Frederick II, Luther, Napoleon have all been suggested.

We have considered two ways of interpreting the book.
The first connects it with its original historical circumstances;
and the second regards it as a detailed prophecy of the
Christian centuries. Two other ways may be mentioned.

Some take the visions as not referring to a particular sequence of events, but as illustrating great principles of the kingdom of God in allegorical form. Each story or picture sets out a part of a great struggle which is continually being enacted. One can see that certain of the passages can be treated in this way, but it is very difficult to interpret the whole book along these lines.

Another method which has had a good deal of support in recent years is known as the futuristic. It regards the main part of the book, from chapter 6 onwards, as referring strictly to the last few years of human history, the few years prior to the return of Christ at the end of the age. On this view, there is certainly a forecast of coming events; but those events, instead of being spread over many centuries, still lie in the future and are all to take place during the short period prior to Christ's return. It is difficult to accept this view, because the book speaks so emphatically of matters which 'must shortly happen' and looks for the return of Jesus in the very near future.

THE STRUCTURE OF THE BOOK

In the first chapter the writer tells us of the vision of Christ which he saw in Patmos; following this are the letters to the seven churches, taking up chapters 2 and 3. Then in chapters 4–22 we have the visions of the future. They begin with the preparatory visions of chapters 4 and 5, in which he sees the 'One who sits on the throne' and the Lamb. The latter receives from God the scroll with *seven seals*. The opening of the seals (6: 1 onwards) is followed by the *seven trumpets* (8: 7 onwards); and then come the *seven bowls* (ch. 16) culminating in the final destruction of Babylon (chs. 17–19). Then follows the thousand years reign, and the Last Judgement (ch. 20); and afterwards the new heaven and earth and the new Jerusalem (chs. 21–2).

There are one or two interludes, and passages which at first seem to hold up the action. But there may well be a purpose in this. The long series of judgements would appal the reader unless there were quieter interludes, especially those which appear to give (out of strict time-sequence) glimpses of the eternal state (7: 9–17, for instance). But there are also sections which have been included for other purposes and we shall examine these when we come to them. The main framework of sevens, provided by the seals, trumpets and bowls, suggests that the book has been constructed according to a definite pattern.

One matter affecting the three series of sevens is this. Some authorities think the writer keeps going back to the beginning again, so that in a sense the seals, trumpets and bowls occupy the same time and are not consecutive. The more usual view, however, is that there is a progressive time-sequence. It may well be that the seventh seal supplies the time of the seven trumpets; and the seventh trumpet marks the period of the seven bowls.

In reading Revelation it is the person steeped in the Old Testament who will understand the allusions and overtones from this source which permeate the book—just as in reading Milton a knowledge of the classics illuminates every line. Ezekiel is specially important, and it is interesting that the outline of this prophecy appears to have suggested the outline of the Revelation. Ezekiel could be divided in the following way:

(1) Ezekiel in captivity sees a vision of God (ch. 1).

(2) Messages to the Jewish people (chs. 2–24).

(3) Judgements upon the nations (chs. 25–32).

(4) The Messianic kingdom (chs. 33–7).

(5) The attack of Gog (chs. 38–9).

(6) A vision of the final glory and peace of the redeemed people of the Lord, closing with the words, 'The Lord is there' (chs. 40–8).

The contents of Revelation correspond:

(1) John in captivity sees a vision of Christ (ch. 1).

(2) Messages to the seven churches (chs. 2–3).

(3) A series of judgements (chs. 6–19) (introduced by visions of God in chs. 4–5).

(4) The Messianic kingdom (20: 1–6).

(5) The attack of Gog and Magog (20: 7–10), followed by the Last Judgement (20: 11–15).

(6) A vision of the final glory and peace of the redeemed people of the Lord in the new Jerusalem. Here again one of the main themes is that 'God himself shall be with them' (chs. 21–2).

It can hardly be accidental that this agreement is so close. John has not only followed a similar framework but he has been greatly influenced by the language of Ezekiel. Other prophets who are important for understanding Revelation are Daniel, Isaiah and Zechariah.

WAS EARLIER MATERIAL USED?

Many authorities believe that the writer made use of earlier material which he incorporated into his book. Genuine visions which he experienced himself may provide the basis of his work, but he also felt free to make use of prophetic fragments which could be woven into his revelation. Some of these may have been productions of his own written years before the complete book took its final shape. This theory helps to explain why some parts fit one date, and other parts another. There is good reason to believe that the book in its final form was published in Domitian's reign (81–96). But certain verses in chapter 11, which imply that the temple in Jerusalem is still standing, seem to belong to the period before the fall of Jerusalem in A.D. 70. And the kings mentioned in 17: 10–11 would suit either the same period, or a little later in Vespasian's reign (69–79). Apocalyptic language is notoriously difficult to interpret, and when the original meaning fails, the words can easily be applied to a later situation. In taking over earlier fragments the apocalyptist would no doubt give his own new interpretation to the words. Again in chapter 12 a pagan story about a woman and a dragon, which has parallels in Greek and Egyptian mythology, has probably been used; and while a Christian meaning has been imposed, this transformation has not been entirely successful.

In view of all this, it is natural that there should be rough edges here and there. Further, if a man is giving utterance to what he has seen in visions, it is to be expected that human language will break down and prove insufficient to give a perfectly satisfying and smooth account. We have only to think of our own dreams. When we are reading about Lewis Carroll's Alice, in a dream of a quite different kind, we do not think it strange if the White Queen turns into a sheep. It is important to remember this sort of atmosphere and not to expect the logical consistency of a closely argued treatise. We must not be disturbed if the Lamb of chapter 5 is also described as a Lion; or if one of the heads of the beast seems to be identified with the beast itself (ch. 17).

WHAT IS THE BOOK'S VALUE?

In great literature, imagery and symbolism can often move us in strange ways and stir us to the depths in a manner we cannot fully understand. This helps to explain the power which the book of Revelation exercises over the reader, even when he lacks a complete understanding of it.

Any large anthology of Bible passages chosen for their beauty is bound to include parts of this book. This is particularly true of the two closing chapters, 21–2, with their visions of the new heaven and earth. An earlier glimpse is also unforgettable, the vast throng robed in white and standing before the throne of God (7: 9–17).

But the most important contribution of all is of course the book's spiritual message, its glowing faith in the unfailing purpose of God and the final victory of righteousness. In the world of today we can still see the marks of the beast, the lust for domination, the claws of cruelty, the pride of possession. But we know that the future belongs to Christ. If Nero could return today to Rome and look for the Vatican gardens where he burned Christians, he would find in their place an enormous church, named after Peter who was probably one of his victims! When the Roman empire fell in the fifth century, the Christian Church remained indestructible. Thus the main theme of Revelation has been proved right by history. John was right in seeing that the future belonged not to the beast but to the Lamb, not to Babylon but to the city of God.

*   *   *   *   *   *   *   *   *   *   *   *   *   *

Prelude

THIS IS THE REVELATION given by God to Jesus **1** Christ. It was given to him so that he might show his servants what must shortly happen. He made it known by sending his angel to his servant John, who, in telling all **2** that he saw, has borne witness to the word of God and to the testimony of Jesus Christ.

Happy is the man who reads, and happy those who **3** listen to the words of this prophecy and heed what is written in it. For the hour of fulfilment is near.

* According to these opening words, God gave this disclosure of the future to Jesus, and Jesus sent an angel to convey it to John.

1. *his servants*. Literally slaves; the same expression occurs later in this verse in the phrase *his servant John*. The word is used throughout the book with various meanings. It may refer (*a*) to Christian prophets, 10: 7; or (*b*) to martyrs, 19: 2; or (*c*) to Christians generally, 22: 3. Here the first meaning is intended. Cf. Amos 3: 7, 'Surely the Lord God will do nothing, but he revealeth his secret unto his servants the prophets'.

what must shortly happen. There can be little doubt that

John believed that the whole of his prophecy would be fulfilled in the near future: this was often the case with apocalyptic writers. *The hour of fulfilment is near* (verse 3).

his angel. Not much is said of angels in the early writings
of the Old Testament (apart from the unique figure of 'the
angel of the Lord'); they tend to become much more prominent in the later books, particularly after the exile in Babylon
(586–538 B.C.). Contact with Babylonian and Persian thought,
in which angelic beings have a vital place, may have stimulated
this Jewish development. Also there was a growing feeling
that God was so great, so utterly beyond man's understanding,
that various forms of mediation between man and God were
necessary. This helps to explain why angels took a more and
more important place. They are particularly prominent in
the apocalyptic writings. Again and again it is through an
angel that God speaks to man; the earlier direct relation had
become obscured. Thus Zechariah speaks repeatedly of 'the
angel that talked with me' (1: 19).

2. *the testimony of Jesus Christ*. An alternative translation is
given in the N.E.B. footnote: 'his testimony to the word of
God and to Jesus Christ'. There is a similar ambiguity when
the phrase is used elsewhere. Here in 1: 2 the translation
given in the text is probably right; God gave the revelation to
Jesus Christ (1: 1) and so it is his testimony.

3. *Happy*. The same Greek word is used in the beatitudes
of Matt. 5: 1–12. There are seven sayings of this kind in
Revelation: 1: 3; 14: 13; 16: 15; 19: 9; 20: 6; 22: 7 (which
virtually repeats 1: 3) and 22: 14. In view of the importance
of the number seven in this book, it may not be an accident
that these new beatitudes add up to this number.

the man who reads...and...those who listen. This refers to
public reading, not individual study, and it indicates that the
work was to be read aloud in the seven churches to which it
was sent (verse 4).

this prophecy. Cf. 22: 7, 10 'the words of prophecy in this
book'. ✳

A Message from Christ
to the Churches

JOHN'S OPENING GREETING

JOHN to the seven churches in the province of Asia. 4
Grace be to you and peace, from him who is and who
was and who is to come, from the seven spirits before his
throne, and from Jesus Christ, the faithful witness, the 5
first-born from the dead and ruler of the kings of the earth.

To him who loves us and freed us from our sins with
his life's blood, who made of us a royal house, to serve 6
as the priests of his God and Father—to him be glory and
dominion for ever and ever! Amen.

Behold, he is coming with the clouds! Every eye shall 7
see him, and among them those who pierced him; and
all the peoples of the world shall lament in remorse. So
it shall be. Amen.

'I am the Alpha and the Omega', says the Lord God, 8
who is and who was and who is to come, the sovereign
Lord of all.

✻ 4. *the seven churches.* These are named in verse 11. The
Greek simply says *Asia*; but the N.E.B. rightly defines this
as *the province of Asia.* (See map, p. xi.)

4–5. Notice the reference here to the Trinity. The Father
is referred to in the words *him who is and who was and who is to
come*; Jesus Christ is directly named; the Holy Spirit corresponds to *the seven spirits before his throne* (see 5: 6, *the seven
spirits of God*). The Holy Spirit 'is regarded here not so much
in his personal unity as in his manifold energies; just as light,

17

being one, does yet in the prism separate itself into its seven colours' (Archbishop Trench, *Letters to Seven Churches*, p. 9). Our Whitsun hymns speak of the seven gifts of the Spirit, and this idea is no doubt derived from Isa. 11: 2, where the spirit of the Lord is also the spirit of wisdom and understanding, counsel and might, knowledge and the fear of the Lord.

5. Jesus is called *the first-born from the dead* also in Col. 1: 18, where the same Greek words are rendered *the first to return from the dead*.

It is notable that Jesus is here described, right at the beginning of the book, as *ruler of the kings of the earth*. Christians at this time were a helpless minority, at the mercy of brutal Roman persecutors. But running through this work is the conviction that in reality the lordship of the universe belongs to 'our Lord and his Christ'. This is shown pictorially in chapter 5 in the vision of the Lamb on the throne.

5–6. The readers are encouraged by the reminder that Jesus loves them, and that they have found release from their sins by his sacrifice. Moreover, in spite of outward appearances they are *a royal house* and they serve as *priests* of God himself. The language is drawn from Exod. 19: 6 where Israel is told, 'ye shall be unto me a kingdom of priests, and an holy nation'. In 1 Pet. 2: 9 the same passage is reflected; the Church inherits the privileges and titles of Israel, since she is the new Israel of God (Gal. 6: 16). The wording of verses 5–6 is the kind of language used in worship, and throughout the book use is made of what may possibly be early Christian hymns. *Amen* (verses 6 and 7), is a Hebrew word meaning 'May it be so' and is used as the termination of a prayer or hymn.

7. This verse gives one of the main themes of the book: the return of Christ and the events associated with it. It also presents a good example of the use of the Old Testament, something we should always be watching for. There are not many direct quotations but the whole wording has an Old

Testament savour. The first part of this verse takes us back to Dan. 7: 13, and the latter part to Zech. 12: 10 ('they shall look unto me whom they have pierced: and they shall mourn for him'). The same two passages are linked together in Matt. 24: 30. The crucifixion story in John 19: 37 also makes use of the Zechariah reference.

The Greek word used here in 1: 7 means 'mourn', but the N.E.B. is probably right in expanding this to *lament in remorse*.

clouds are often associated with manifestations of God (e.g. at Sinai, Exod. 19: 16), but here they come from Dan. 7: 13 where the 'one like unto a son of man' comes 'with the clouds of heaven'.

8. *Alpha* is the first letter of the Greek alphabet and *Omega* the last. We should say A and Z. It is another way of saying 'first and last and all-inclusive'. For the thought, the repeated phrase of Isaiah may be recalled, 'I am the first, and I am the last; and beside me there is no God' (44: 6). Here in Rev. 1: 8 it is *the Lord God* who is given this description; in 22: 13 the same phrase is apparently applied to Jesus; see also 1: 17. ✳

A VISION OF THE GLORIFIED CHRIST

I, John, your brother, who share with you in the suffering 9 and the sovereignty and the endurance which is ours in Jesus—I was on the island called Patmos because I had preached God's word and borne my testimony to Jesus. It 10 was on the Lord's day, and I was caught up by the Spirit; and behind me I heard a loud voice, like the sound of a trumpet, which said to me, 'Write down what you see on 11 a scroll and send it to the seven churches: to Ephesus, Smyrna, Pergamum, Thyatira, Sardis, Philadelphia, and Laodicea.' I turned to see whose voice it was that spoke 12 to me; and when I turned I saw seven standing lamps of gold, and among the lamps one like a son of man, robed 13 down to his feet, with a golden girdle round his breast.

14 The hair of his head was white as snow-white wool, and
15 his eyes flamed like fire; his feet gleamed like burnished
brass refined in a furnace, and his voice was like the sound
16 of rushing waters. In his right hand he held seven stars,
and out of his mouth came a sharp two-edged sword;
and his face shone like the sun in full strength.

17 When I saw him, I fell at his feet as though dead. But
he laid his right hand upon me and said, 'Do not be
18 afraid. I am the first and the last, and I am the living one;
for I was dead and now I am alive for evermore, and I
19 hold the keys of death and Hades. Write down therefore
what you have seen, what is now, and what will be
hereafter.

20 'Here is the secret meaning of the seven stars which you
saw in my right hand, and of the seven lamps of gold: the
seven stars are the angels of the seven churches, and the
seven lamps are the seven churches.

* Several of the great prophets began their ministry with an
overwhelming vision of the glory of God. Isaiah, in the account
of his call (Isa. 6), describes how he saw the Lord 'high and
lifted up'. The first chapter of Ezekiel is another example.
So it is with John the Seer; at the opening of his prophecy
he describes a vision of the triumphant Christ in his glory. In
a way, his authority as a prophet is grounded in this vision
and in the commission given him by his Lord (verses 19–20).

9. These words are usually taken to imply that the writer
was a prisoner on Patmos and had been sentenced because of
his faith in Jesus. There is some evidence that prisoners on this
island had to work in the quarries; it may have been a kind of
labour camp. Visitors are still shown the traditional cave
where John lived when he saw these visions.

10. *the Lord's day*. The only instance of this phrase in the New Testament. Later it was the usual name given to Sunday or the first day of the week. The Greek word for *Lord's* is *Kuriake*, from which 'church' and 'kirk' are derived. Paul uses the same adjective in the phrase 'the Lord's Supper' (I Cor. II: 20). I Cor. 16: 2 refers to 'every Sunday' and it was evidently from early days the time when the Christians gathered for worship.

caught up by the Spirit. Physically John was a prisoner on Patmos, but mentally he was transported into a different region of reality. In his ecstasy he hears a voice and sees a vision.

11. The speaker, who turns out to be Jesus himself, bids John write the substance of his vision and send it to *the seven churches* of the province of Asia, here named in the order in which a traveller would come to them (see map p. xi). Something will be said of these places individually when we come to the seven letters of chapters 2 and 3.

12. Notice the recurring sevens. Already we have had the seven spirits, the seven churches, and we shall find the number seven a main factor of the pattern underlying the whole work. The Jews regarded it as a sacred number and it is prominent in the Old Testament (e.g. seven days of the week, seven-branched candlestick).

lamps of gold. Many golden objects appear in these chapters; e.g. the golden girdle of the next verse, crowns of gold (4: 4), golden bowls (5: 8). Gold was the most appropriate metal to suggest splendour and glory.

13. Again the phrases are drawn from the Old Testament. For *one like a son of man* see Dan. 7: 13; and the angel of Dan. 10: 5 was 'girded with pure gold'. *Son of man* simply means man, here and in Dan. 7.

14–15. Dan. 7: 9 describes the ancient of days as having hair 'like pure wool'; the eyes which *flamed like fire* and the feet *like burnished brass* take us again to the angel of Dan. 10: 6 ('his eyes as lamps of fire, and his arms and his feet like in colour to burnished brass'). Cf. also Ezek. 1: 7, 'the colour of burnished brass'.

Some have explained *the sound of rushing waters* by recalling the breakers of the Aegean Sea dashing upon the coast of Patmos; but it is more likely that John is reproducing Ezek. 43: 2, 'his voice was like the sound of many waters'.

16. The *seven stars* are interpreted in verse 20. The *sharp two-edged sword* symbolizes the penetrating power of the divine word—hence it comes *out of his mouth*; see Heb. 4: 12 where the word of God 'cuts more keenly than any two-edged sword', and Isa. 49: 2: 'he hath made my mouth like a sharp sword'.

The seven letters of chapters 2 and 3 mostly begin by referring to one or other of the items given in this description (1: 12–16). But we must not allow attention to phrases to rob us of the magnificence of the description as a whole.

17 gives the reaction of John to this overwhelming vision of Christ. Comparison may be made with the feeling of Ezekiel (1: 28, 'I fell upon my face') or Isaiah (6: 5, 'I am a man of unclean lips') or of Peter in the presence of Christ (Luke 5: 8, 'leave me, sinner that I am!').

18. Jesus is not only *alive for evermore* but he holds the keys of human destiny.

Hades was originally (in Homer) the name of the Greek god of the underworld; in course of time the abode of the god came to be known as Hades. In the New Testament it is used to represent the realm of the dead (see Acts 2: 31.) It must not be confused with hell (Gehenna), the ultimate place of punishment, called in this book 'the lake of fire' (19: 20).

20. *angels*. This may mean the pastors of the seven churches. But at this particular period it is more likely that it refers to literal angels, each church standing under the patronage of an angel-protector. In Daniel each nation has its own angel, and it may be that the idea was extended to other communities such as local churches. In chapters 2 and 3, John is told to write 'To the angel of the church at Ephesus' and so on.

the seven lamps stand for churches. The words of Jesus in
Matt. 5: 14–16 may be recalled, 'You are light for all the
world.... And you, like the lamp, must shed light among your
fellows.'

THE SEVEN LETTERS

The letters to the seven churches make an interesting study
(chs. 2–3). Their structure should be observed, as this is
worked out with care. Practically all of them contain:

(*a*) Some phrase drawn from the vision of Christ in
chapter 1.

(*b*) The words 'I know' (in several cases, 'I know all your
ways') leading to an estimate of the Church's condition.

(*c*) Words of rebuke or encouragement.

(*d*) A promise for those who are victorious, who stand fast
in the ordeal of persecution.

(*e*) The saying, 'Hear, you who have ears to hear, what the
Spirit says to the churches!' In the last four letters this comes
at the end, but in the others just before the promise.

Some of the letters, as we shall see, mention matters
peculiar to the area of the church in question and thus appear
to show a personal knowledge of local conditions. ✳

THE LETTER TO EPHESUS

'To the angel of the church at Ephesus write: **2**
   ' "These are the words of the One who holds the seven
stars in his right hand and walks among the seven lamps
of gold: I know all your ways, your toil and your forti-   2
tude. I know you cannot endure evil men; you have put
to the proof those who claim to be apostles but are not,
and have found them false. Fortitude you have; you have   3
borne up in my cause and never flagged. But I have this   4
against you: you have lost your early love. Think from   5
what a height you have fallen; repent, and do as you once

did. Otherwise, if you do not repent, I shall come to you
6 and remove your lamp from its place. Yet you have this
in your favour: you hate the practices of the Nicolaitans,
7 as I do. Hear, you who have ears to hear, what the Spirit
says to the churches! To him who is victorious I will give
the right to eat from the tree of life that stands in the
Garden of God."

* * *

✳ *Ephesus* was a key city in the province of Asia; it stood at a
strategic point and several vital roads converged there. Paul
spent three years at Ephesus and regarded it as a command-
ing centre which could influence a wide area. One of his
adventures there will be remembered from Acts 19. The
temple of Diana was included as one of the seven wonders
of the world; pieces of the actual building which once
stood at Ephesus may be seen today in the British Museum in
London.

The letter recalls two details of the vision of chapter 1 with
the words *the One who holds the seven stars in his right hand and
walks among the seven lamps of gold* (verse 1; see 1: 16 and
1: 12-13). The Church is praised on four counts: (*a*) for the
matters mentioned in 2, *I know all your ways, your toil and
your fortitude*; (*b*) for the way in which it tests those who claim
to be apostles, 2; (*c*) for fortitude again, 3; (*d*) and later in the
letter for its refusal to tolerate the false teaching of the
Nicolaitans, 6. In between these words of praise is the stern
rebuke of 4 and 5.

2. *apostles*. The word means literally 'missionaries' and
does not refer here to 'the twelve'. These pseudo-apostles or
false missionaries appear to be the Nicolaitans of 6.

4. *you have lost your early love*. This reminds us of the charge
brought against Israel in the Old Testament, that she had
forgotten 'the kindness of thy youth, the love of thine
espousals' (Jer. 2: 2; cf. Hos. 2: 14-16). The orthodoxy of this
church was insufficient without love.

24

5. The threat expressed in these words about the removal of the lamp means that they are in danger of disappearing. The light of Christian witness which once burned at Ephesus has actually been quenched; Ephesus itself is a ruin.

6. *Nicolaitans.* This cannot be interpreted with certainty, as no such sect is mentioned elsewhere in the records of the first century; but they are sometimes identified with the Balaamites of 14–15. We shall see the particular practices of the Balaamites when we come to these verses.

7. *the tree of life that stands in the Garden of God.* This can be understood only by recalling the story of the garden in Gen. 3. The final verse of that chapter records that after man's disobedience and expulsion, the cherubim with flaming swords stood at the east of the garden of Eden to bar the way to the tree of life. But in Christ Paradise is restored, and the way to the tree of life is open; see 22: 14, *those who wash their robes clean...have the right to the tree of life.* ✳

THE LETTER TO SMYRNA

'To the angel of the church at Smyrna write: 8

' "These are the words of the First and the Last, who was dead and came to life again: I know how hard pressed 9 you are, and poor—and yet you are rich; I know how you are slandered by those who claim to be Jews but are not—they are Satan's synagogue. Do not be afraid of the 10 suffering to come. The Devil will throw some of you into prison, to put you to the test; and for ten days you will suffer cruelly. Only be faithful till death, and I will give you the crown of life. Hear, you who have ears to 11 hear, what the Spirit says to the churches! He who is victorious cannot be harmed by the second death."

✳ 8. *Smyrna* was an important city, and still is; its modern name is Izmir. Being a port, it was the outlet for the trade of an extensive area. It is not mentioned in the Acts of the Apostles. Again the letter begins with words taken from the vision of Christ in chapter 1.

9. *poor—and yet you are rich*. The church of Laodicea was in the opposite situation: 'You say, "How rich I am!"...In fact...you are the most pitiful wretch, poor, blind, and naked' (3: 17). Material wealth can go with spiritual poverty; and the converse is equally true.

those who claim to be Jews. It is known that the Jews were numerous at Smyrna; since the Christian Church claims to be the 'Israel of God' (Gal. 6: 16) it is here denied that they are true Jews. They may have their synagogue worship, but *they are Satan's synagogue*. This hostile attitude of the writer is to be explained by the fact that Jews sometimes joined in stirring up persecution against the Christians, as the Thessalonian Jews, for example, did at Beroea on Paul's first journey through Macedonia (Acts 17: 13).

10. *ten days*, a round number, meaning a short period. The approaching persecution though short would be sharp; it would involve imprisonment for some and death for others. And so they are bidden to be *faithful till death*, i.e. to the point of dying for the name of Christ.

the crown of life. For this term see also 3: 11 and Jas. 1: 12. Smyrna was famous for its games; and the figure of speech here may be borrowed from the wreath awarded to athletic victors.

11. *the second death*. This is explained in 21: 8; the first death is natural physical death, but for some its sequel is judgement and retribution. ✳

THE LETTER TO PERGAMUM

12 'To the angel of the church at Pergamum write:

'"These are the words of the One who has the sharp
13 two-edged sword: I know where you live; it is the place where Satan has his throne. And yet you are holding fast

to my cause. You did not deny your faith in me even at the time when Antipas, my faithful witness, was killed in your city, the home of Satan. But I have a few matters 14 to bring against you: you have in Pergamum some that hold to the teaching of Balaam, who taught Balak to put temptation in the way of the Israelites. He encouraged them to eat food sacrificed to idols and to commit fornication, and in the same way you also have some who hold 15 the doctrine of the Nicolaitans. So repent! If you do not, 16 I shall come to you soon and make war upon them with the sword that comes out of my mouth. Hear, you who 17 have ears to hear, what the Spirit says to the churches! To him who is victorious I will give some of the hidden manna; I will give him also a white stone, and on the stone will be written a new name, known to none but him that receives it."

✻ 12. *Pergamum.* This also was an important city about 15 miles from the sea. It is interesting that our word 'parchment' is derived from this name. When supplies of papyrus from Egypt were cut off, a king of Pergamum in the second century B.C. made extensive use of animal skin as writing material and this came to be known as *pergamena.* This city was the first centre of emperor-worship in Asia Minor; and this may explain the description *the place where Satan has his throne* (verse 13).

13. *Antipas, my faithful witness, was killed in your city.* Nothing is known of this martyr beyond what is said here. The Greek word for witness is *martus*; and as so many faithful witnesses were killed for their faith the word came to mean martyr. In the New Testament it always means witness; but after the middle of the second century it could mean either witness or martyr.

14. Balaam was the prophet hired by Balak, king of Moab,

to curse Israel; but his utterances always came out as blessings! (Num. 22–4). In Num. 31: 16 Balaam is blamed for the sin of the Israelites who committed fornication with Moabite women. He was regarded in New Testament times as a forerunner of all corrupt teachers, as in 2 Pet. 2: 15–16 and Jude 11. In Num. 25: 1–2 (the immediate sequel of the Balaam chapters) fornication with the daughters of Moab is associated with idolatry; the Israelites shared in the heathen worship by eating the flesh of animals sacrificed to the gods of Moab. Curiously enough these two problems are found together several times in the New Testament. Two of the four prohibitions mentioned in Acts 15: 29 are 'to abstain from meat that has been offered to idols...and from fornication'. It is possible that this rule of the Jerusalem council was known to the churches of Asia. Acts 15: 28 says, in the words leading up to the fourfold injunction, that the decision was 'to lay no further burden upon you beyond these essentials'; in Rev. 2: 24 the words *on you I will impose no further burden* are connected with the two matters now under discussion, as the problem involved Thyatira as well as Pergamum. Again, in 1 Cor. 6–10 Paul deals at length with these two problems.

A good deal of the meat offered for sale in most cities had first been slaughtered ceremonially in the name of some pagan god, so Christians could only avoid eating meat sacrificed to idols by becoming vegetarians or making other arrangements for slaughter. But a more serious complication arose when they were invited to a feast by a friend; if the feast were held in a heathen temple (as in 1 Cor. 8: 10) there was a danger of being involved in idolatry and of compromising the faith.

15. *the Nicolaitans* whom we first met in 2: 6 evidently encouraged the two practices mentioned.

17. *the hidden manna.* Manna was the 'bread from heaven' which the Israelites ate in the wilderness (Exod. 16). Some of it was stored in a golden pot and kept near or within the ark in the Tabernacle (Exod. 16: 33–4; Heb. 9: 4). The Jews

believed that in the last days, the days of the Messiah, the gift of manna would be repeated; in John 6 Jesus fulfils this expectation in his offer of the Bread of Life.

a white stone. A number of explanations have been put forward, but none of them is entirely satisfactory. It is said that there was a custom of giving a white pebble as a ticket of admission to a feast; the promise would then mean the right of sharing in the heavenly feast. Again, a white stone was associated with special happiness; Pliny speaks of a glad day being marked with a white stone. But neither of these suggestions accounts for the name written on the stone.

Some have found a connexion with the Urim and Thummim used for reaching decisions (Exod. 28: 30); these were probably stones used as lots, and were kept in the high priest's breastplate or pouch. G. F. Moore, a great authority on Jewish matters, illustrates this method of divination by referring to the ancient Arabs, who at times used arrows for this purpose; then (without any thought of Rev. 2: 17) he goes on to say that 'other objects, such as white pebbles, were also used' (*Encyclopaedia Biblica*, col. 5236). Now, there was a Jewish tradition (mentioned in a Targum, an Aramaic paraphrase of scripture) that the name of God was inscribed on the Urim and Thummim. This would provide an attractive way of explaining both the white stone and the new name. In 3: 12 the Lord speaks of 'my own new name'; and this may agree with the reference here.

known to none but him that receives it. This could easily mean: none but him that receives the stone.

One advantage of the above explanation is that it links together the manna and the stone. 'The hidden manna and the white stone are not merely united in time, belonging both to the wilderness period of the history of God's people; but they are united as both representing high-priestly prerogatives, which the Lord should at length impart to all his people, kings and priests to God, as he will then have made them all' (Trench, *Letters to Seven Churches*, p. 137). *

THE LETTER TO THYATIRA

18 'To the angel of the church at Thyatira write:

' "These are the words of the Son of God, whose eyes flame like fire and whose feet gleam like burnished brass:
19 I know all your ways, your love and faithfulness, your good service and your fortitude; and of late you have
20 done even better than at first. Yet I have this against you: you tolerate that Jezebel, the woman who claims to be a prophetess, who by her teaching lures my servants into
21 fornication and into eating food sacrificed to idols. I have given her time to repent, but she refuses to repent of
22 her fornication. So I will throw her on to a bed of pain, and plunge her lovers into terrible suffering, unless they
23 forswear what she is doing; and her children I will strike dead. This will teach all the churches that I am the searcher of men's hearts and thoughts, and that I will reward each
24 one of you according to his deeds. And now I speak to you others in Thyatira, who do not accept this teaching and have had no experience of what they like to call the deep secrets of Satan; on you I will impose no further
25 burden. Only hold fast to what you have, until I come.
26 To him who is victorious, to him who perseveres in doing my will to the end, I will give authority over the
27 nations—that same authority which I received from my Father—and he shall rule them with an iron rod, smashing
28 them to bits like earthenware; and I will give him also
29 the morning star. Hear, you who have ears to hear, what the Spirit says to the churches!" '

* *Thyatira* was the least important of the seven cities; it was 40 miles south-east of Pergamum. It will be remembered that a woman named Lydia from this city opened her house to Paul when he was at Philippi; she is described as 'a dealer in purple fabric from the city of Thyatira' (Acts 16: 14). There were several trade guilds here, and it is possible that the abuses mentioned arose from Christians participating in the pagan feasts held by these guilds, feasts which at times ended in licentious behaviour.

20. *Jezebel* is the name given to some woman belonging to this church who used her prophetic gifts and influence to foster these abuses. Her real name is unknown. The original Jezebel was the wife of Ahab, King of Israel, and as a foreign princess she introduced idolatrous and degrading ways into Israel, which were opposed by Elijah (1 Kings 16–18).

22–3. *her lovers...and her children.* This may refer to church members who through her influence had embraced the Nicolaitan teaching, rather than to actual children.

24. *the deep secrets of Satan.* Paul speaks of 'the depths of God's own nature' (1 Cor. 2: 10); and we know that language of this kind was used by false teachers who called themselves Gnostics, people who claimed to find salvation by secret knowledge (Greek *gnosis* = knowledge). John affirms that their teaching is in fact Satanic depths, and not divine— the opposite of what they claimed. Some of the Gnostics maintained that as the soul alone was divine, and the body was essentially evil, any behaviour which the body resorted to (including fornication) could not damage the soul. The Christian, they said, was emancipated from the moral law. It seems that the Nicolaitan doctrine was of this type.

27. The words come from Ps. 2: 9.

28. *I will give him also the morning star.* The morning star (which is the same as the evening star and the planet Venus) is the herald of dawn. It could stand for the spirit of hope. See also 22: 16. ✳

THE LETTER TO SARDIS

3 'To the angel of the church at Sardis write:

' "These are the words of the One who holds the seven spirits of God, the seven stars: I know all your ways; that though you have a name for being alive, you are dead.
2 Wake up, and put some strength into what is left, which must otherwise die! For I have not found any work of
3 yours completed in the eyes of my God. So remember the teaching you received; observe it, and repent. If you do not wake up, I shall come upon you like a thief, and you
4 will not know the moment of my coming. Yet you have a few persons in Sardis who have not polluted their clothing. They shall walk with me in white, for so they
5 deserve. He who is victorious shall thus be robed all in white; his name I will never strike off the roll of the living, for in the presence of my Father and his angels I will
6 acknowledge him as mine. Hear, you who have ears to hear, what the Spirit says to the churches!"

* *Sardis* was about 30 miles from Thyatira. It was the city of the famous and wealthy ruler Croesus (sixth century B.C.) and in his day it was the capital of the kingdom of Lydia. The church is not blamed for any specific sin, but it has become sleepy and half-dead. It is called upon to wake up and to watch. Rather curiously, in the preceding centuries Sardis had twice been captured through lack of vigilance. Carelessness in keeping watch had led to the capture of the citadel, the acropolis, by the enemy. It looks as though this casual spirit had crept into the church. Like the enemies in their past history, Christ will come upon them *like a thief* (verse 3). Cf. Matt. 24: 43–4.

4. Compromise with evil is spoken of under the imagery of

soiled garments. Those who avoid this contamination will finally walk with their Lord in white robes.

5. *I will acknowledge him as mine.* Literally, I will acknowledge his name. A contrast may be intended here between 'striking off' the name, and reading it out from *the roll of the living.* Cf. Luke 12: 8 'everyone who acknowledges me before men, the Son of Man will acknowledge before the angels of God'. ✶

THE LETTER TO PHILADELPHIA

'To the angel of the church at Philadelphia write: 7

' "These are the words of the holy one, the true one, who holds the key of David; when he opens none may shut, when he shuts none may open: I know all your 8 ways; and look, I have set before you an open door, which no one can shut. Your strength, I know, is small, yet you have observed my commands and have not disowned my name. So this is what I will do: I will make those of 9 Satan's synagogue, who claim to be Jews but are lying frauds, come and fall down at your feet; and they shall know that you are my beloved people. Because you have 10 kept my command and stood fast, I will also keep you from the ordeal that is to fall upon the whole world and test its inhabitants. I am coming soon; hold fast what you 11 have, and let no one rob you of your crown. He who is 12 victorious—I will make him a pillar in the temple of my God; he shall never leave it. And I will write the name of my God upon him, and the name of the city of my God, that new Jerusalem which is coming down out of heaven from my God, and my own new name. Hear, 13 you who have ears to hear, what the Spirit says to the churches!"

* 7. *Philadelphia*. The name means brotherly love; but the city was actually named after its founder Attalus II Philadelphus, a king of Pergamum (died 138 B.C.). It was 28 miles south-east of Sardis.

the key of David does not figure in the description in chapter 1. The first five letters have used up most of the phrases suitable for this kind of quotation, and so in letters 6 and 7 supplementary descriptions are given. There are keys mentioned in 1: 18, but they are the keys of death and Hades. The present passage is derived from Isa. 22: 22, 'And the key of the house of David will I lay upon his shoulder; and he shall open, and none shall shut; and he shall shut, and none shall open'. In Isaiah the words are applied to Eliakim, the treasurer of the royal household. But here they describe Christ himself who alone admits men to the new city of David, the new Jerusalem. His key is used for other purposes also, as the next verse suggests.

8. The *open door* is apparently a door of opportunity for witness, and is to be explained by such passages as 1 Cor. 16: 9. Literally, the Greek in the Corinthian passage speaks of a door that has been opened, but the N.E.B. renders it as 'a great opportunity has opened for effective work'.

9. For *Satan's synagogue* see 2: 9 and the note.

10. *the ordeal that is to fall upon the whole world* is probably to be identified with 'the great ordeal' of 7: 14 and the 'distress such as never has been until now' of Mark 13: 19–20 (from Dan. 12: 1). It means a definite period of time coinciding with the $3\frac{1}{2}$ years of Antichrist's rule, as in Rev. 13: 5–10. To be kept from this ordeal does not mean that they will escape but by the power of Christ they will be kept spiritually secure, i.e. free from sin.

12. *I will make him a pillar*. For the imagery see Gal. 2: 9, 'those reputed pillars of our society'.

Philadelphia suffered from frequent earthquakes; again and again the inhabitants had to flee from it and take refuge in the open country. It has been suggested that there is a reference

to this in the words *he shall never leave it* (lit. 'he shall go out
no more'). But this is perhaps reading too much into the
words.

*the name of my God...the name of the city...my own new
name.* The high priest had the words 'Holy to the Lord' on
his forehead on a plate of gold (Exod. 28: 36–8); this may
explain the imagery here. Each believer has high-priestly
dignity; 'his servants shall worship him...and bear his name
on their foreheads' (22: 4).

The *new Jerusalem* is seen coming down from heaven in
chapter 21 where a full description of it is given.

For the *new name* see 19: 12 and 2: 17. ✻

THE LETTER TO LAODICEA

'To the angel of the church at Laodicea write: 14

' "These are the words of the Amen, the faithful and
true witness, the prime source of all God's creation: I 15
know all your ways; you are neither hot nor cold. How
I wish you were either hot or cold! But because you are 16
lukewarm, neither hot nor cold, I will spit you out of my
mouth. You say, 'How rich I am! And how well I have 17
done! I have everything I want in the world.' In fact,
though you do not know it, you are the most pitiful
wretch, poor, blind, and naked. So I advise you to buy 18
from me gold refined in the fire, to make you truly rich,
and white clothes to put on to hide the shame of your
nakedness, and ointment for your eyes so that you may
see. All whom I love I reprove and discipline. Be on 19
your mettle therefore and repent. Here I stand knocking 20
at the door; if anyone hears my voice and opens the door,
I will come in and sit down to supper with him and he
with me. To him who is victorious I will grant a place 21

on my throne, as I myself was victorious and sat down
22 with my Father on his throne. Hear, you who have ears
to hear, what the Spirit says to the churches!" '

✻ *Laodicea* was 10 miles from Colossae, and is mentioned by
Paul in Col. 4: 16. He evidently wrote a letter to the Christians
there, but it has been lost, unless (as some think) it is the one
we call the epistle to the Ephesians. The very word Laodicea
has come to stand for the lukewarm and the half-hearted who
are described in 15–17.

14. *the Amen.* This is a Hebrew word familiar to us through
its use at the end of prayers. But its meaning here, somewhat
different from the liturgical use, is brought out by the words
which immediately follow, *the faithful and true witness.* The
title may have been suggested by Isa. 65: 16 where 'God of
truth' would be literally translated 'God of Amen'.

the prime source of all God's creation. This conception of the
work of the Son of God in creation is in harmony with what
is said in John 1: 1–18 and 1 Cor. 8: 6, 'Jesus Christ, through
whom all things came to be'.

17–18. Notice the contrast with the condition of the
church at Smyrna (2: 9) which imagined it was so poor and
yet was in reality rich. Proud Laodicea and the Christians
within it were ignorant of their real condition: *though you do
not know it, you are the most pitiful wretch, poor, blind, and naked.*
For their poverty they must obtain *gold* from their Lord, for
their blindness *ointment,* and for their nakedness *white clothes.*
It can hardly be accidental that three things for which
Laodicea was famous were (1) its wealth; it was a banking
centre and stood on a highway of oriental trade; (2) its wool;
and (3) its flourishing medical school. But it is from Christ
that they must obtain (1) the true wealth, *gold...to make
you truly rich;* (2) clothes to hide their shame; but whereas
Laodicea produced wool of a raven blackness, Christ offers
them *white clothes;* and (3) *ointment for your eyes so that you
may see.* There was a well-known Phrygian powder used for

eye complaints and this would no doubt be employed at the Laodicean medical school. But spiritual blindness can be cured by Christ alone.

20. These words are often, quite appropriately, used in reference to Christ's call to the individual soul. One cannot help recalling Holman Hunt's famous painting, The Light of the World. But the words are addressed to the Laodicean church. Is Jesus knocking on the door of a church, because they had kept him outside despite their imagined success? He is rather appealing to each individual within the community.

I will...sit down to supper with him and he with me. These words could refer to the future, but it is better to regard them as applicable to the present also; this would fit their use in the Communion Service, and the use of the phrase *if anyone* would favour this interpretation. ✷

The Opening of the Sealed Book

THE VISION OF GOD

AFTER THIS I looked, and there before my eyes was a 4 door opened in heaven; and the voice that I had first heard speaking to me like a trumpet said, 'Come up here, and I will show you what must happen hereafter.' At once I was caught up by the Spirit. There in heaven 2 stood a throne, and on the throne sat one whose appear- 3 ance was like the gleam of jasper and cornelian; and round the throne was a rainbow, bright as an emerald. In a 4 circle about this throne were twenty-four other thrones, and on them sat twenty-four elders, robed in white and wearing crowns of gold. From the throne went out 5

flashes of lightning and peals of thunder. Burning before
the throne were seven flaming torches, the seven spirits
6 of God, and in front of it stretched what seemed a sea of
glass, like a sheet of ice.

In the centre, round the throne itself, were four living
7 creatures, covered with eyes, in front and behind. The
first creature was like a lion, the second like an ox, the
third had a human face, the fourth was like an eagle in
8 flight. The four living creatures, each of them with six
wings, had eyes all over, inside and out; and by day and
by night without a pause they sang:

> 'Holy, holy, holy is God the sovereign Lord of all, who
> was, and is, and is to come!'

9 As often as the living creatures give glory and honour
and thanks to the One who sits on the throne, who lives
10 for ever and ever, the twenty-four elders fall down
before the One who sits on the throne and worship him
who lives for ever and ever; and as they lay their crowns
before the throne they cry:

11   'Thou art worthy, O Lord our God, to receive glory
     and honour and power, because thou didst create all
     things; by thy will they were created, and have their
     being!'

* Chapters 4–22 are occupied with coming events, but before
they are developed in detail there is a vision of God (ch. 4)
and of the Lamb (ch. 5). The two chapters are parts of one
tremendous scene; chapter 4 shows us God as Creator,
chapter 5 God as Redeemer, the idea of redemption being
expressed in the figure of the Lamb. The climax of chapter 4
is verse 11, *Thou art worthy, O Lord our God...thou didst create*

all things. The climax of chapter 5 is verse 12, *Worthy is the Lamb, the Lamb that was slain.*

1. *Come up here.* In his vision the seer is transported to heaven.

3. *There in heaven stood a throne.* This represents in symbol the sovereignty of God. In spite of the apparent victory of evil on earth, behind the shadows there is a throne. The last word is always with God. One recalls the great saying of Jeremiah: 'A glorious throne, set on high from the beginning, is the place of our sanctuary' (17: 12). The word *throne* occurs in almost every chapter of Revelation, over forty times; it sounds throughout the book like the ground-bass of a great organ theme.

Notice the great reticence in describing the one sitting *on the throne…like the gleam of jasper and cornelian.* No shape of any kind is indicated, although in 5: 1 'the right hand of the One who sat on the throne' is mentioned. This almost complete absence of any description is in contrast to Dan. 7: 9 with its ancient of days with hair like wool (a detail transferred to Jesus in Rev. 1: 14), and Ezek. 1: 26, 'and upon the likeness of the throne was a likeness as the appearance of a man upon it above'.

4. The meaning of the *twenty-four elders* is not certain. There is a possible clue in 21: 13–14; in the new Jerusalem there are two sets of twelve: the gates correspond to the twelve tribes of Israel and the foundation-stones to the twelve apostles of the Lamb. This combines into a unity the Old Testament and the New; the old 'people of God' of pre-Christian times, and the new Israel of which the apostles are foundation members. Thus we reach the number 24. It may well be that the twenty-four elders are intended to convey the same idea.

5. The lightning and thunder are reminiscent of the great 'theophany' (i.e. appearance of God) at Sinai, Exod. 19: 16.

Again there is mention of *the seven spirits of God*; see 1: 4 and 5: 6.

6. The *sea of glass* may be explained by considering a larger question. Several times in the book mention is made of a heavenly temple; and since the present chapter is dominated by the thought of the throne, the reader wonders how these two are related. Does the imagery of heaven change from a royal court to a temple, and back again? This would not be impossible; both types of imagery are needed to bring out the full reality and one fades into the other, as in a dream. But there is another explanation, which is preferable.

Isaiah tells us in chapter 6 of his prophecy, 'I saw the Lord, sitting upon a *throne*...and his train filled the *temple*'. He thus combines in one picture the throne and the temple. There was a sense in which the ark at the inmost shrine of the earthly temple was thought of as God's throne. Ps. 80: 1 speaks of God sitting upon the cherubim; and in the description of the tabernacle, the place of the divine presence is above the mercy-seat between the two cherubim (Exod. 25: 22). We know that John was strongly influenced by Isaiah's vision; in fact, in this very chapter the *six wings* (verse 8) of the living creatures come straight from Isa. 6: 2. This strongly supports the view that in Revelation the dwelling-place of God is pictured as a combination of temple and royal court. This would be in agreement with 1: 6, a passage which combines together the kingly and the priestly; the people of God are 'a royal house, to serve as the priests'.

This matter has been dwelt upon because it governs our understanding of much of the imagery used throughout the book. It may also help us to interpret the *sea* mentioned here. In Solomon's temple there was an enormous basin of water which was called a 'sea' (1 Kings 7: 23–6). It may be that the glassy sea which John saw in the heavenly sanctuary corresponds to this.

6–8. The *four living creatures* are suggested by Ezekiel's vision in his first chapter; and as we have already noticed, the *six wings* come from Isa. 6 and its description of the seraphim. Ezek. 1: 10 speaks of the faces of the four living creatures he saw, though in his interpretation each one of them had four faces: 'As for the likeness of their faces, they had the face of a man; and they four had the face of a lion on the right side; and they four had the face of an ox on the left side; they four had also the face of an eagle.' In later times these four creatures were connected with the four Gospels, the man with Matthew, the lion with Mark, the calf with Luke and the eagle with John, but this is of no relevance to the original meaning. Here they probably stand for the created world in its energy and variety.

For the *eyes* see Ezek. 10: 12, where the four angelic beings are 'full of eyes'.

The song is reminiscent of the cry of the seraphim in Isa. 6: 3: 'Holy, holy, holy, is the Lord of hosts: the whole earth is full of his glory.' This emphasis upon worship is characteristic of the book. Again and again it bursts into song, and it may preserve for us here and there fragments of early hymns. Some of the great hymn-writers (Wesley, Watts) turned constantly to this book for their phrases and images (e.g. Watts's hymn, 'Come, let us join our cheerful songs').

9–11. The song of the living creatures leads on to that of the twenty-four elders. ✽

THE LAMB AND THE SEALED BOOK

Then I saw in the right hand of the One who sat on the **5** throne a scroll, with writing inside and out, and it was sealed up with seven seals. And I saw a mighty angel **2** proclaiming in a loud voice, 'Who is worthy to open the scroll and to break its seals?' There was no one in heaven **3** or on earth or under the earth able to open the scroll or to look inside it. I was in tears because no one was **4** found who was worthy to open the scroll or to look inside it. But one of the elders said to me: 'Do not weep; for **5** the Lion from the tribe of Judah, the Root of David, has won the right to open the scroll and break its seven seals.'

6 Then I saw standing in the very middle of the throne, inside the circle of living creatures and the circle of elders, a Lamb with the marks of slaughter upon him. He had seven horns and seven eyes, the eyes which are the seven

7 spirits of God sent out over all the world. And the Lamb went up and took the scroll from the right hand of the

8 One who sat on the throne. When he took it, the four living creatures and the twenty-four elders fell down before the Lamb. Each of the elders had a harp, and they held golden bowls full of incense, the prayers of God's

9 people, and they were singing a new song:

> 'Thou art worthy to take the scroll and to break its seals, for thou wast slain and by thy blood didst purchase for God men of every tribe and language,
> 10 people and nation; thou hast made of them a royal house, to serve our God as priests; and they shall reign upon earth.'

11 Then as I looked I heard the voices of countless angels. These were all round the throne and the living creatures and the elders. Myriads upon myriads there were,

12 thousands upon thousands, and they cried aloud:

> 'Worthy is the Lamb, the Lamb that was slain, to receive all power and wealth, wisdom and might, honour and glory and praise!'

13 Then I heard every created thing in heaven and on earth and under the earth and in the sea, all that is in them, crying:

'Praise and honour, glory and might, to him who sits
on the throne and to the Lamb for ever and ever!'

And the four living creatures said, 'Amen', and the elders 14
fell down and worshipped.

* In chapter 4 the emphasis was upon God as Creator. Now
comes the theme of man's redemption from sin. The presence
of the Lamb, *with the marks of slaughter upon him*, on the
throne of the universe, speaks of the sovereignty of sacrifice
and the victory of love. But the vision is also closely related
to the following chapters. The sealed book which the Lamb
is to open holds the secrets of the future, and its contents are
unfolded in the sequel.

1. *a scroll, with writing inside and out*. In pre-Christian times
there were no books with pages which could be turned.
Writing was upon single sheets, or if this was insufficient,
upon lengths of papyrus or parchment which could be
rolled up in scroll fashion. It was customary to write on only
one side, naturally the inner side, so that all the writing would
be concealed when the papyrus was rolled up. But occasionally both sides were used, as here. Ezekiel, early in his ministry,
was given a scroll 'written within and without' (2: 9–10); it
contained lamentations, mourning and woe.

seven seals. These must have been arranged in an unusual
way; for in the succeeding chapters the breaking of each seal
meant that a further portion of the scroll of doom could be
read.

5. Christ is first announced as *the Lion from the tribe of
Judah, the Root of David*. The former idea is connected with
Gen. 49: 9 where Judah is described as a lion's whelp. The
latter comes from Isa. 11: 1 where the coming Messiah is
indicated in the words 'a shoot out of the stock of Jesse, and
a branch out of his roots'. (Jesse was, of course, David's
father.)

6. *standing in the very middle of the throne*. The N.E.B. gives

an alternative translation in the footnote, 'standing between the throne, with the four living creatures, and the elders'. But the translation given in the text is to be preferred. In 3: 21 Jesus says, 'I myself was victorious and sat down with my Father on his throne'. It is impossible to envisage with accuracy the scene described in chapter 5. We are in the realm of symbol. We should think probably of a dais with more than one occupant if we are to make the language intelligible.

a Lamb. This is one of the most frequent titles applied to Jesus in this book (nearly thirty times), and it demands special attention. Jesus is called a Lamb in John 1: 29, 36; and the same idea is implied in 1 Pet. 1: 19. For the Old Testament background of this term we should take into account the Passover lamb, and also 'the servant of God' in Isa. 53: 7, who was led as a lamb to the slaughter. It is sometimes claimed that Jewish apocalypses spoke of the Messiah as a lamb, or a militant ram, but the evidence for this is uncertain. It would certainly suit the somewhat martial deeds attributed to the Lamb in certain chapters of Revelation if we regarded him as the bell-wether (or leading sheep) of God's flock. But the note of sacrifice is more important here in chapter 5; the Lamb bears upon him the marks of slaughter.

The Greek word used for Lamb throughout Revelation is interesting; it is not the word used in John 1 and 1 Pet. 1 (*amnos*) but *arnion*. We have already noted the contrast between the Lamb and the beast which is so vital to our understanding of the book; and as the word used for beast is *therion*, John may have preferred *arnion* for Lamb because of the similar ending. The beast does not come on the scene before chapter 11; but in the latter half of the book we shall follow the struggle between them, the *arnion* versus the *therion*.

seven horns and seven eyes suggest that the Lamb is strong and all-knowing. The influence of Zech. 4: 10 may be traced here: 'these seven, which are the eyes of the Lord; they run to and fro through the whole earth.'

8. *incense, the prayers of God's people.* Ps. 141: 2 makes a similar comparison, 'Let my prayer be set forth as incense before thee'.

9. *by thy blood didst purchase for God.* The blood of Christ is a vivid way of referring to his death on the cross. The idea of purchase may seem strange at first. But anything which is obtained at great cost may be described as purchased. When the missionary Hannington was about to be killed as a martyr in Africa he said, 'Go and tell king Mwanga that I have purchased the road to Uganda with my blood'. He meant he had won it at the cost of his life. In a similar way, by his cross Jesus has won us for God's service, secured us in such a way that we acknowledge that we belong to him. As Paul put it, 'You do not belong to yourselves; you were bought at a price' (1 Cor. 6: 19–20).

The blood of Christ is associated also with liberation (1: 5), cleansing (7: 14), and victory (12: 11, where the N.E.B. rendering is 'By the sacrifice of the Lamb', but the word 'blood' is in the Greek).

men of every tribe and language, people and nation. The universality of the Church is stressed in these words. The same four terms are used concerning the beast in 13: 7.

10. *a royal house, to serve our God as priests.* As in 1: 6 there is an echo of Exod. 19: 5–6.

12. *Worthy is the Lamb, the Lamb that was slain.* This song in celebration of redemption answers to the song of creation in the previous chapter, 'Thou art worthy, O Lord our God' (4: 11). It should be noted that the same kind of worship is offered to Christ as to God the Father.

13. First the elders sing (verses 8–10), then countless angels (verse 11), and finally every created thing in the four regions of the universe brings the swelling song to a climax.

Before we leave this chapter, a further note on its significance may be added. We can think of nothing more helpless than a lamb. It is true that the Lamb here has some remarkable features and is also described as the Lion of Judah. Nevertheless it is a lamb and it bears the marks of sacrifice. Later on in the book we shall meet the beast, and the fearful description of it in chapter 13 combines the savagery of leopard, bear and lion. In any contest between these two, it would seem that the Lamb has no chance. And yet as the story unfolds the victory goes to the Lamb, who stands for goodness and sacrificial love. This conception of the Lamb on the throne of the universe is one of the most sublime in the Bible. It suggests that love is the strongest power in the world.

It must be admitted that the rest of the book has not brought out in a consistent way the great truth of this vision. In the Fourth Gospel it is by the cross itself that Jesus wins the world; his suffering and his victory go together (John 12: 31-3), and it is this which is symbolized in the vision of Rev. 5. If only John the seer had found some way of maintaining this principle throughout, what a great work this would be! But instead, the victory is finally envisaged as springing from sheer force; the Lamb changes to the rider on the white horse, sprinkled by the blood of his foes, smiting the nations with a sharp sword and gaining supremacy by slaughter and divine omnipotence (19: 11-21).

In actual fact the contest between the Church and the empire was won by spiritual weapons. The Church endured ten great persecutions, from Nero to Diocletian (fourth century) and survived them all. As a church historian has said, in that fierce struggle only one side was armed and that was the side that lost (H. B. Workman, *Persecution in the Early Church*, pp. 240 f.). It was the way of the Lamb that was vindicated. ✻

THE FIRST FOUR SEALS

6 Then I watched as the Lamb broke the first of the seven seals; and I heard one of the four living creatures say in a
2 voice like thunder, 'Come!' And there before my eyes

was a white horse, and its rider held a bow. He was given a crown, and he rode forth, conquering and to conquer.

When the Lamb broke the second seal, I heard the 3 second creature say, 'Come!' And out came another 4 horse, all red. To its rider was given power to take peace from the earth and make men slaughter one another; and he was given a great sword.

When he broke the third seal, I heard the third creature 5 say, 'Come!' And there, as I looked, was a black horse; and its rider held in his hand a pair of scales. And I 6 heard what sounded like a voice from the midst of the living creatures, which said, 'A whole day's wage for a quart of flour, a whole day's wage for three quarts of barley-meal! But spare the olive and the vine.'

When he broke the fourth seal, I heard the voice of the 7 fourth creature say, 'Come!' And there, as I looked, was 8 another horse, sickly pale; and its rider's name was Death, and Hades came close behind. To him was given power over a quarter of the earth, with the right to kill by sword and by famine, by pestilence and wild beasts.

* The seven seals are passed over fairly rapidly. Six of them are dealt with in this chapter; but the seventh does not appear until 8: 1. The opening of each seal is the signal for some disaster to begin. Later on, further calamities come with the blowing of the seven trumpets and the pouring out of the seven bowls. We should therefore be prepared for a whole series of painful happenings; and it must be admitted that these central chapters, 6–16, do not convey as much to a modern reader as chapters 1–5 and have not the same enduring value.

The first four seals form a group and are connected with four horsemen. These have some connexion with the visions of Zech. 1 and 6. In Zech. 1: 7–17 horses of various colours are described, representing patrols sent to and fro in the earth to bring back a report of its conditions. In Zech. 6: 1–8 four chariots are mentioned drawn by horses of four different colours, though more than four horses are involved; these too are sent to patrol the earth. Three of the colours (red, black, white) match three of the horses in Rev. 6. But the meaning of the horses in our passage is quite different. 'The four horsemen of the Apocalypse' stand for kinds of disasters which are to come on the earth in the immediate future.

The other two seals mentioned in this chapter are not associated with horsemen. But if we examine the six items we find that they roughly correspond to the scheme of Mark 13: 7–9, 24–5 (and the parallels in Matt. 24 and Luke 21), a part of a passage sometimes known as the Little Apocalypse, in which war is followed by international strife, earthquakes, famine and heavenly portents, somewhat as in the present passage.

1. Each of the four horsemen is summoned to action by one of the four living creatures.

2. The first horseman stands for War.

3–4. The second appears to be similar in its symbolism, but perhaps the wider area suggested, *to take peace from the earth*, implies a fuller degree of international strife.

5–6. The black horse represents Famine. A whole day's work brings in only *a quart of flour*, or *three quarts of barley-meal*; yet, ironically, luxuries are plentiful in the shape of oil and wine.

7–8. The fourth horse of *sickly pale* colour denotes Death and Hades. *A quarter of the earth* is involved here, and among the causes of death are *pestilence and wild beasts*. ✻

THE FIFTH AND SIXTH SEALS

9 When he broke the fifth seal, I saw underneath the altar the souls of those who had been slaughtered for God's
10 word and for the testimony they bore. They gave a

great cry: 'How long, sovereign Lord, holy and true, must it be before thou wilt vindicate us and avenge our blood on the inhabitants of the earth?' Each of them 11 was given a white robe; and they were told to rest a little while longer, until the tally should be complete of all their brothers in Christ's service who were to be killed as they had been.

Then I watched as he broke the sixth seal. And there 12 was a violent earthquake; the sun turned black as a funeral pall and the moon all red as blood; the stars in 13 the sky fell to the earth, like figs shaken down by a gale; the sky vanished, as a scroll is rolled up, and every 14 mountain and island was moved from its place. Then 15 the kings of the earth, magnates and marshals, the rich and the powerful, and all men, slave or free, hid themselves in caves and mountain crags; and they called out to 16 the mountains and the crags, 'Fall on us and hide us from the face of the One who sits on the throne and from the vengeance of the Lamb.' For the great day of their 17 vengeance has come, and who will be able to stand?

✻ 9–11. The opening of the fifth seal discloses the souls of the martyred dead under the heavenly altar, crying out impatiently for the avenging of their blood, '*How long, sovereign Lord?*' This echoes the language of such passages as Ps. 79: 5, 10: 'How long, O Lord?...Let the revenging of the blood of thy servants which is shed be known among the heathen in our sight.' It should be frankly recognized that this is not a Christian prayer. It is in marked contrast with the prayer of Jesus at Calvary, 'Father, forgive them; they do not know what they are doing' (Luke 23: 34) and the words of Stephen the first martyr (Acts 7: 60).

The idea of souls *underneath the altar* is difficult. The only altar specifically identified in Revelation is the altar of incense (8: 3–4); and since incense was compared to prayer (5: 8) it may be that the souls here mentioned made their prayer in proximity to this heavenly altar. It is not stated that this was their permanent home. There is a saying of the Jewish rabbis that 'the souls of the righteous are kept safely under the throne of glory'.

11. *until the tally should be complete.* Certain Jewish writings taught that the age would end when a certain number of souls had been born, or a fixed number of the elect had been reached. In 2 Esdras 4: 35–6 the souls of the righteous in the beyond ask, 'How long are we here? when cometh the fruit of the threshing time of our reward? And unto them Jeremiel the archangel gave answer, and said, Even when the number is fulfilled of them that are like unto you.'

12–17. The sixth seal brings terrible portents in the heavens, the falling of stars, the rolling up of the sky; and with these goes the moving of mountains. For the imagery see Isa. 34: 4.

16. *they called out to the mountains...Fall on us and hide us.* This passage, like Jesus' words at Luke 23: 30, shows the influence of Hos. 10: 8, 'they shall say to the mountains, Cover us; and to the hills, Fall on us'. Verses 14–17 seem to suggest that the folding up of the heavens discloses to men in some visible fashion the threatening features of God and the Lamb; but it is not certain that the words must be taken in this literal sense. *

THE SEALING OF THE SERVANTS OF GOD

7 After this I saw four angels stationed at the four corners of the earth, holding back the four winds so that no wind 2 should blow on sea or land or on any tree. Then I saw another angel rising out of the east, carrying the seal of the living God; and he called aloud to the four angels

who had been given the power to ravage land and sea:
'Do no damage to sea or land or trees until we have set 3
the seal of our God upon the foreheads of his servants.'
And I heard the number of those who had received the 4
seal. From all the tribes of Israel there were a hundred
and forty-four thousand: twelve thousand from the tribe 5
of Judah, twelve thousand from the tribe of Reuben,
twelve thousand from the tribe of Gad, twelve thousand 6
from the tribe of Asher, twelve thousand from the tribe
of Naphtali, twelve thousand from the tribe of Manasseh,
twelve thousand from the tribe of Simeon, twelve 7
thousand from the tribe of Levi, twelve thousand from
the tribe of Issachar, twelve thousand from the tribe 8
of Zebulun, twelve thousand from the tribe of Joseph,
and twelve thousand from the tribe of Benjamin.

✻ 1–3. The four winds are held back from their destructive
task; but nothing is said again about these winds at any later
stage. This is one of the reasons for suspecting that an earlier
fragment has been incorporated here.

2–3. To understand the 'sealing', it is necessary to remember a passage of the Old Testament; and once again it is
to Ezekiel that we must turn. In Ezek. 9, before the judgement upon the unfaithful nation takes place, an angel with
an ink-horn is told to go through the city and to 'set a mark
upon the foreheads of the men that sigh and that cry for all the
abominations that be done in the midst thereof' (9: 4). Here
in Rev. 7 a certain number, 12,000 from each of the twelve
tribes, are marked on their foreheads. This suggests that they
would be immune from the approaching judgements.

4–8. Two puzzling points about the twelve tribes must be
mentioned.

(a) Of the twelve tribes, the ten which made up the
northern kingdom called 'Israel', had virtually disappeared

from history some centuries before New Testament times. The southern kingdom of Judah and Benjamin had continued in various forms; its people were known as Jews (Judahites). The Levites held no territory and they also survived in good numbers and from them came the priests and attendants who ministered in the temple. But the 'lost ten tribes' had been absorbed into the surrounding nations, some of them contributing to the mixture which made up the Samaritans. How then are we to understand the twelve tribes in the present passage? The answer is that according to Jewish belief, the lost tribes were still in some unknown hiding place and would return before the end; this point is mentioned in a number of apocalypses, and it is evidently adopted here. 2 Esdras 13: 40–8 speaks of the return of the ten tribes from beyond the Euphrates: 'Then dwelt they there until the latter time; and now when they begin to come again....'

(*b*) The other point concerns the names of the tribes. For the purpose of land division in the old days the number twelve had been made up without the Levites by dividing the tribe of Joseph into two parts named after his sons, Manasseh and Ephraim. But in the present list Levi is included (verse 7) and we should therefore expect Joseph without any mention of his sons. But strangely, in addition to Joseph (verse 8) his son Manasseh is included (verse 6) but not Ephraim; and stranger still there is no mention of Dan. One suggestion, that comes to us from very early times, is that Dan is omitted because it was thought by certain people that Antichrist would come from this tribe. Another suggestion is that Dan originally stood in verse 6 following Naphtali; a scribe's error turned Dan into Man and this was later taken to be an abbreviation (Man.) and was expanded into Manasseh. The latter explanation is preferable.

No further mention of these 144,000 is made in the book, unless we identify them with a company of the same number in 14: 1; and it is possible that 7: 1–8 is a piece of Jewish tradition which the writer has taken over. He would understand it as a reference to Jewish Christians. There was a continuing belief that when Elijah returned before the end (cf. Mal. 4: 5–6) he would convert the Jews to the Christian faith. It may well be that John held this belief; and as we shall see later, one of the two witnesses in Rev. 11 is probably Elijah. The 144,000 could then be regarded as his converts. Augustine wrote, 'That this great and mighty prophet Elijah shall convert the Jews unto Christ before the judgement, by expounding unto them the law, is most commonly believed and taught by us Christians' (*City of God* 20: 29).

The multitude in the latter part of the chapter is, in contrast, made up of Gentile Christians *from every nation* (verse 9). ✳

THE VAST THRONG BEFORE THE THRONE

After this I looked and saw a vast throng, which no one 9 could count, from every nation, of all tribes, peoples, and languages, standing in front of the throne and before the Lamb. They were robed in white and had palms in their hands, and they shouted together: 10

'Victory to our God who sits on the throne, and to the Lamb!'

And all the angels stood round the throne and the elders 11 and the four living creatures, and they fell on their faces before the throne and worshipped God, crying: 12

'Amen! Praise and glory and wisdom, thanksgiving and honour, power and might, be to our God for ever and ever! Amen.'

Then one of the elders turned to me and said, 'These 13 men that are robed in white—who are they and from where do they come?' But I answered, 'My lord, you 14 know, not I.' Then he said to me, 'These are the men who

have passed through the great ordeal; they have washed
their robes and made them white in the blood of the
15 Lamb. That is why they stand before the throne of God
and minister to him day and night in his temple; and he
16 who sits on the throne will dwell with them. They shall
never again feel hunger or thirst, the sun shall not beat
17 on them nor any scorching heat, because the Lamb who
is at the heart of the throne will be their shepherd and will
guide them to the springs of the water of life; and God
will wipe all tears from their eyes.'

✴ The great multitude of martyrs in heaven are shown in the
glory which they will ultimately enjoy. The vision is not
given in strict time-sequence but is a preliminary glimpse of
the bliss of those who endure unto death. It is a habit of the
writer to introduce from time to time a peaceful interlude,
as a relief from the series of horrors with which he is so largely
concerned. Another purpose for introducing the heavenly
scene at this point is to strengthen and encourage those who
were being persecuted.

> And when the strife is fierce, the warfare long,
> Steals on the ear the distant triumph song,
> And hearts are brave again, and arms are strong.

14. *the great ordeal.* This refers to a definite time of acute
suffering and is to be identified with that spoken of in 3: 10;
see note.

white in the blood of the Lamb. A literal-minded reader may
find it hard to see how blood can make anything white; but
the blood is a way of referring to the cross of Christ and it is a
fact that through the cross multitudes have had their soiled
lives purified and have been assured of God's forgiveness.

15. Again there is a reference to the heavenly temple. These
martyrs form a priestly community offering their worship.

16–17. The words are taken from Isa. 49: 10, 'They shall

not hunger nor thirst; neither shall the heat nor sun smite them: for he that hath mercy on them shall lead them, even by the springs of water shall he guide them'. This passage shows the writer's skilful way of weaving together Old Testament phrases; his closing words come from Isa. 25: 8, 'and the Lord God will wipe away tears from off all faces'; cf. Rev. 21: 4.

17. *the Lamb* has become a title for 'the Messiah', or 'the Son of God', and so it is not really a mixed metaphor to say that the Lamb becomes a shepherd or has a bride (21: 2). ✶

THE SEVENTH SEAL

Now when the Lamb broke the seventh seal, there was **8** silence in heaven for what seemed half an hour. Then I 2 looked, and the seven angels that stand in the presence of God were given seven trumpets.

Then another angel came and stood at the altar, hold- 3 ing a golden censer; and he was given a great quantity of incense to offer with the prayers of all God's people upon the golden altar in front of the throne. And from the 4 angel's hand the smoke of the incense went up before God with the prayers of his people. Then the angel took 5 the censer, filled it from the altar fire, and threw it down upon the earth; and there were peals of thunder, lightning, and an earthquake.

✶ 1-2. Under the seventh seal, at a time when the judgements might be expected to end, there are seven trumpets. In a similar way when we come to the seventh trumpet, seven bowls follow.

This *silence* is like the ominous calm before a terrific storm.

the seven angels that stand in the presence of God. The definite article suggests that we should regard these as the seven archangels; they were Gabriel (who says in Luke 1: 19, 'I stand in attendance upon God'), Michael, Raphael, Uriel, Raguel, Saraqael, and Remiel (=Jeremiel, mentioned in the note on 6: 11). These are the names given in Enoch 20. Only Michael and Gabriel are named in the Bible. Raphael is one of the principal characters in the book of Tobit (in the Apocrypha) and he says, 'I am Raphael, one of the seven holy angels, which...go in before the glory of the Holy One' (12: 15).

3–5. On the link between *incense* and *prayers* see 5: 8 and the note. The imagery comes from *the golden altar* of incense in the temple at Jerusalem. The priests took it in turn to carry the incense into the holy place in a censer every day. They also took with them into this building a fire-pan filled with hot coals from the altar of burnt-offering. (*This* altar was of course in the open air in the court.) They heaped the coals on the golden altar and then poured the incense on them; clouds of fragrant smoke resulted, filling the holy place. The father of John the Baptist, Zechariah, was on one famous occasion allotted the task of entering the sanctuary to 'offer the incense' (Luke 1: 9) in this way.

We have already noted in earlier chapters that Jews and Christians believed that there was a heavenly counterpart of the earthly temple; its imagery runs through the book. But it seems that only one altar is associated with the heavenly temple and that is the altar of incense, *the golden altar*, mentioned also in verse 5. There would be no purpose or meaning in an altar of burnt-offering in heaven; the sacrifice of Christ was offered on earth, and there could hardly be anything in heaven answering to animal sacrifices. The heavenly sanctuary is prominent in the epistle to the Hebrews also.

the golden altar is *in front of the throne*. Once again the temple imagery is combined with that of the royal court. So it was in the previous chapter; the saints 'stand before the throne of God and minister to him...in his temple' (7: 15). The epistle to the Hebrews also combines the priestly and the royal; Christ is the high priest, but he also sits 'at the right hand of Majesty on high' (1: 3). ✳

The Powers of Darkness Conquered

THE FIRST FOUR TRUMPETS

6 THEN THE seven angels that held the seven trumpets prepared to blow them.

7 The first blew his trumpet; and there came hail and fire mingled with blood, and this was hurled upon the earth. A third of the earth was burnt, a third of the trees were burnt, all the green grass was burnt.

8 The second angel blew his trumpet; and what looked like a great blazing mountain was hurled into the sea. A 9 third of the sea was turned to blood, a third of the living creatures in it died, and a third of the ships on it foundered.

10 The third angel blew his trumpet; and a great star shot from the sky, flaming like a torch; and it fell on a third of the rivers and springs. The name of the star 11 was Wormwood; and a third of the water turned to wormwood, and men in great numbers died of the water because it had been poisoned.

12 The fourth angel blew his trumpet; and a third part of the sun was struck, a third of the moon, and a third of the stars, so that the third part went dark and a third of the light of the day failed, and of the night.

13 Then I looked, and I heard an eagle calling with a loud cry as it flew in mid-heaven: 'Woe, woe, woe to the inhabitants of the earth when the trumpets sound which the three last angels must now blow!'

⁎ 6–7. As with a number of these trumpets, it is a third of the creation that is affected, *a third of the earth ... and a third of the trees*.

8. It has been suggested that at Patmos John could see a volcanic island (Thera) in action and this may have inspired the vision of a *blazing mountain...hurled into the sea*. When the Thera volcano erupted in 1573 the sea around it was tinted orange with the iron oxide. Such a phenomenon might produce the impression that *the sea was turned to blood*.

10. *a great star*. Evidently a 'shooting star' or meteor.

11. *Wormwood* is a plant whose root has a bitter taste. It is referred to a number of times in the Old Testament and always its bitterness is implied; it is associated with gall in Deut. 29: 18; Jer. 9: 15 and elsewhere.

13. *Woe, woe, woe*. The three woes correspond to the last three trumpets; see 9: 12, 'The first woe has now passed. But there are still two more to come'. ✳

THE FIFTH TRUMPET

9 Then the fifth angel blew his trumpet; and I saw a star that had fallen to the earth, and the star was given the
2 key of the shaft of the abyss. With this he opened the shaft of the abyss; and from the shaft smoke rose like smoke from a great furnace, and the sun and the air were
3 darkened by the smoke from the shaft. Then over the earth, out of the smoke, came locusts, and they were
4 given the powers that earthly scorpions have. They were told to do no injury to the grass or to any plant or tree, but only to those men who had not received the seal of
5 God on their foreheads. These they were allowed to torment for five months, with torment like a scorpion's
6 sting; but they were not to kill them. During that time these men will seek death, but they will not find it; they will long to die, but death will elude them.

7 In appearance the locusts were like horses equipped for

battle. On their heads were what looked like golden
crowns; their faces were like human faces and their hair 8
like women's hair; they had teeth like lions' teeth, and 9
wore breastplates like iron; the sound of their wings was
like the noise of horses and chariots rushing to battle;
they had tails like scorpions, with stings in them, and in 10
their tails lay their power to plague mankind for five
months. They had for their king the angel of the abyss, 11
whose name, in Hebrew, is Abaddon, and in Greek,
Apollyon, or the Destroyer.

The first woe has now passed. But there are still two 12
more to come.

✻ Few commentators have been able to find much of spiritual
or literary value in this chapter. We have the impression that
the writer has to fill out his numerical scheme of sevens
somehow; and so horror is piled upon horror.

1. Stars were sometimes identified with angels as in the
book of Enoch, and this explains how a star can be given a
key with which to open up the shaft of the underworld abyss.

2–5. Under the fifth trumpet there is a plague of locusts,
somewhat similar to that described so graphically in Joel 2;
and in several places the influence of this prophet may be
traced. Joel had described the flying locusts as darkening the
sky, 'The earth quaketh before them; the heavens tremble:
the sun and the moon are darkened, and the stars withdraw
their shining' (2: 10). So it is here; the smoke, out of which
the locusts come, darkens the sun and the air.

4. This clearly looks back to 7: 3, where the servants of
God receive his *seal...upon the foreheads*.

6. It is not explained how these men are debarred from
suicide.

7–8. *the locusts were like horses*. This idea comes from Joel
2: 4 where the same comparison is made, 'The appearance
of them is as the appearance of horses'.

59

they had teeth like lions' teeth; cf. Joel 1: 6, 'his teeth are the teeth of a lion'.

It is true that the locust has a face somewhat resembling that of a horse, and its thorax is like a *breastplate*; but the rest of the description is bizarre indeed: golden crowns on their heads, *human faces and their hair like women's hair*. This last point may possibly refer to the antennae of the locust, which an Arabian proverb compares to a maiden's hair.

11. *the angel of the abyss* is given a Hebrew name *Abaddon* and a Greek name *Apollyon*. The two words mean roughly the same, though strictly speaking 'Abaddon' means 'destruction' and 'Apollyon' 'the destroyer'. 'Abaddon' is mentioned in the Old Testament with the same meaning as 'Sheol' (= Hades); Job 28: 22 is a good example of its Old Testament use, 'Destruction [Abaddon] and Death say, We have heard a rumour thereof with our ears'. This occurs in the great poem on Wisdom; it will be noticed that Abaddon is personified as in the present passage. *

THE SIXTH TRUMPET

13 The sixth angel then blew his trumpet; and I heard a voice coming from between the horns of the golden altar that
14 stood in the presence of God. It said to the sixth angel, who held the trumpet: 'Release the four angels held
15 bound at the great river Euphrates!' So the four angels were let loose, to kill a third of mankind. They had been held ready for this moment, for this very year and month,
16 day and hour. And their squadrons of cavalry, whose count I heard, numbered two hundred million.

17　This was how I saw the horses and their riders in my vision: They wore breastplates, fiery red, blue, and sulphur-yellow; the horses had heads like lions' heads, and
18 out of their mouths came fire, smoke, and sulphur. By

these three plagues, that is, by the fire, the smoke, and the sulphur that came from their mouths, a third of mankind was killed. The power of the horses lay in their mouths, 19 and in their tails also; for their tails were like snakes, with heads, and with them too they dealt injuries.

The rest of mankind who survived these plagues still 20 did not abjure the gods their hands had fashioned, nor cease their worship of devils and of idols made from gold, silver, bronze, stone, and wood, which cannot see or hear or walk. Nor did they repent of their murders, their 21 sorcery, their fornication, or their robberies.

✳ The sixth trumpet releases four angels who, in readiness for this precise moment, had been held bound at the river Euphrates. They lead an immense horde of horses and riders. Like the locusts of the previous section they are described in an unusual fashion; the horses have lions' heads and stings in their tails, and the tails are like snakes, complete with snakes' heads. A third of the human race is wiped out at this stage. The remainder, however, still persist obdurately in their idolatrous and sinful ways.

14. *Release the four angels held bound*. There seems to be no connexion with the four angels of 7: 2 'who had been given the power to ravage land and sea' but were prevented from operating until the sealing had taken place (7: 3). These earlier angels were 'stationed at the four corners of the earth' (7: 1), but the present four are stationed, or rather *held bound*, at the river Euphrates. This, so some suggest, reflects the constant fear of Parthian invasion, a standing menace to the Roman empire. The Euphrates is mentioned again in 16: 12 and 'the kings from the east' appear in the same verse.

16–19. The *squadrons of cavalry*, advancing in stupendous numbers, are described in almost demonic terms. ✳

THE ANGEL WITH THE LITTLE SCROLL

10 Then I saw another mighty angel coming down from heaven. He was wrapped in cloud, with the rainbow round his head; his face shone like the sun and his legs

2 were like pillars of fire. In his hand he held a little scroll unrolled. His right foot he planted on the sea, and his

3 left on the land. Then he gave a great shout, like the roar of a lion; and when he shouted, the seven thunders spoke.

4 I was about to write down what the seven thunders had said; but I heard a voice from heaven saying, 'Seal up what the seven thunders have said; do not write it down.'

5 Then the angel that I saw standing on the sea and the land

6 raised his right hand to heaven and swore by him who lives for ever and ever, who created heaven and earth and the sea and everything in them: 'There shall be no more

7 delay; but when the time comes for the seventh angel to sound his trumpet, the hidden purpose of God will have been fulfilled, as he promised to his servants the prophets.'

8 Then the voice which I heard from heaven was speaking to me again, and it said, 'Go and take the open scroll in the hand of the angel that stands on the sea and the land.'

9 So I went to the angel and asked him to give me the little scroll. He said to me, 'Take it, and eat it. It will turn your stomach sour, although in your mouth it will taste

10 sweet as honey.' So I took the little scroll from the angel's hand and ate it, and in my mouth it did taste sweet as honey; but when I swallowed it my stomach turned sour.

11 Then they said to me, 'Once again you must utter prophecies over peoples and nations and languages and many kings.'

✻ This short chapter is an introduction to the blowing of the seventh trumpet, which is mentioned in verse 7 but is not sounded until we reach 11: 15.

1–2. The dramatic descent from heaven of a mighty angel is vividly described, *the rainbow round his head*, his face shining like the sun, his legs like pillars of fire, one foot planted on the sea and the other on the land.

The *little scroll* in the angel's hand is dealt with in the closing verses, 8–10.

3–4. Reference to *the seven thunders* might lead one to expect another series of woes: the first thunder, the second and so on. But this idea is not developed, and as we shall see, the seven trumpets are in due course followed by the seven bowls (ch. 16).

The sealing spoken of here shows the influence of Dan. 12: 4 and 9; but as the message of the thunders was not written down it is difficult to see how sealing can enter into this situation.

5. The same chapter of Daniel has no doubt suggested the language here; a man clothed in linen, clearly an angel, 'held up his right hand and his left hand..., and sware by him that liveth for ever' (Dan. 12: 7).

6. It is interesting to observe the new translation here. The older versions gave the impression that the writer was making some profound philosophical statement, 'Time shall be no more'. But there is no doubt that the present translation is correct, *There shall be no more delay*. The word 'delay' instead of 'time' was given in the R.V. margin.

7. *the hidden purpose of God*. Literally 'the mystery of God', his secret counsel made known to *the prophets*.

8–10. To understand what is said about *the little scroll* we must turn to Ezekiel once again. In Ezek. 3: 1–3 the prophet is told to eat a little scroll and he finds it as honey for sweetness; it had been passed to him by 'a hand' (2: 9) and it contained 'written therein lamentations, and mourning, and woe' (2: 10). Similarly in Rev. 10, John is given a scroll from the hand of an angel, and while like Ezekiel's scroll it was sweet to his taste, when swallowed it turned his stomach sour (verse 10) because of the dreadful dooms written upon it.

Mention of this little scroll may well be a hint that the writer is about to use material taken from a different source. This would explain certain unusual features in chapters 11 and 12. ✻

THE TWO WITNESSES

11 I was given a long cane, a kind of measuring-rod, and told: 'Now go and measure the temple of God, the altar,
2 and the number of the worshippers. But have nothing to do with the outer court of the temple; do not measure that; for it has been given over to the Gentiles, and they will trample the Holy City underfoot for forty-two
3 months. And I have two witnesses, whom I will appoint to prophesy, dressed in sackcloth, all through those
4 twelve hundred and sixty days.' These are the two olive-trees and the two lamps that stand in the presence of the
5 Lord of the earth. If anyone seeks to do them harm, fire pours from their mouths and consumes their enemies; and thus shall the man die who seeks to do them harm.
6 These two have the power to shut up the sky, so that no rain may fall during the time of their prophesying; and they have the power to turn water to blood and to strike
7 the earth at will with every kind of plague. But when they have completed their testimony, the beast that comes up from the abyss will wage war upon them and will
8 defeat and kill them. Their corpses will lie in the street of the great city, whose name in allegory is Sodom, or
9 Egypt, where also their Lord was crucified. For three days and a half men from every people and tribe, of every language and nation, gaze upon their corpses and refuse

them burial. All men on earth gloat over them, make 10
merry, and exchange presents; for these two prophets
were a torment to the whole earth. But at the end of the 11
three days and a half the breath of life from God came into
them; and they stood up on their feet to the terror of all
who saw it. Then a loud voice was heard speaking to 12
them from heaven, which said, 'Come up here!' And
they went up to heaven in a cloud, in full view of their
enemies. At that same moment there was a violent earth- 13
quake, and a tenth of the city fell. Seven thousand people
were killed in the earthquake; the rest in terror did
homage to the God of heaven.

The second woe has now passed. But the third is soon 14
to come.

✴ With this chapter the scene changes to Jerusalem. A brief
review of the earlier part of the book shows that in chapter 1
we were in Patmos, in chapters 2–3 in Asia with the seven
churches, in chapters 4–5 in heaven; chapters 6–10 were mostly
concerned with the world as a whole. But mention of the
temple (verses 1–2) and the city *where also their Lord was
crucified* (verse 8) indicates that Jerusalem is now the centre of
interest. A number of commentators have taken the view
that this section has been taken over from an earlier writing.

1–2. These verses seem on the surface to belong to a period
before the fall of Jerusalem in A.D. 70. They could have been
written at the beginning of the Jewish War (66–70) or when
events were working towards it. They suggest that a promise
is being given that, although the outer court of the temple will
be taken by the Roman attackers, the temple itself will remain
secure. Actually the temple did fall, as Jesus had foretold
(Mark 13: 2); it was burnt out and has never been rebuilt.
This makes it difficult to think that these verses could have
been written after the disaster of 70. John may have included

them here because they were a part of the passage concerning the two witnesses, and no doubt he had his own interpretation of their meaning.

3–6. *two witnesses.* Several explanations of the identity of these two have been offered; but verse 6 suggests that one of them is Elijah, who was expected to return to the earth before the end in accordance with the promise of Mal. 4: 5–6. Shutting up the sky *so that no rain may fall* is just what Elijah did in 1 Kings 17: 1. The power to turn water to blood similarly suggests Moses and his action in Exod. 7: 17–21; mention of *every kind of plague* also recalls the ten plagues which Moses brought upon Egypt.

The return of Elijah before the end of the age was part of Jewish expectation, and it is referred to a number of times in the Gospels (e.g. Mark 9: 11–13). In one sense John the Baptist was held to be the fulfilment of this promise, but the return of Elijah personally was still looked for. Occasionally in Jewish and Christian writings other forerunners of the Messiah are mentioned, Enoch for example. As, according to Old Testament story, neither Elijah nor Enoch died, it may have been felt that their work on earth was not yet ended; they would come back to complete their task. Some authorities have suggested that the two witnesses here are Elijah and Enoch. But there is evidence that Moses was also expected to return (there was something unusual about *his* departure from the earth too, and legend had been busy adding further details to the Bible story), and as we have seen, the deeds of Moses are reflected in verse 6. A saying attributed to a first-century Jewish teacher declares that God promised Moses to bring him back to the earth with Elijah when the time was ready. This whole matter may have some connexion with the Transfiguration story, when Moses and Elijah were seen with Jesus. Also Deut. 18: 15–18 promised the coming of a prophet like unto Moses; this description certainly fits Rev. 11: 6*b*.

3. The 1260 days are dealt with below.

4. *the two olive-trees and the two lamps.* This comes from

Zech. 4, where the two olive-trees correspond to Zerubbabel and Joshua, who lived about 520 B.C., at the time of the return from the Babylonian exile. The work of the two witnesses is appropriately illustrated from this earlier period when two servants of God stood forth as leaders.

7. *the beast that comes up from the abyss.* The first mention of this sinister character. He is dealt with more fully in chapter 13 and the details given there show that the great figure of evil expected at the end of the age had become merged with the belief in Nero's return. This will be referred to again under chapter 13. The language of 11: 7 is probably John's. If in this section he is drawing upon an earlier writing, it is likely that it gave at this point some other description of Antichrist which has now been brought into line with the conception of Nero returning from hell.

8. *the great city, whose name in allegory is Sodom, or Egypt.* This is a strange description for Jerusalem. But two Old Testament passages help to explain it. Isaiah addressed the leaders of Judah and Jerusalem as 'rulers of Sodom', implying that the people resembled that notorious city (Isa. 1: 10; cf. 3: 9). Ezekiel condemned Jerusalem for retaining evil ways 'brought from the land of Egypt' (Ezek. 23: 27).

THE THREE AND A HALF YEARS

Mention has been made in verse 2 of a period of 42 months, and in verse 3 of 1260 days (i.e 42 months of 30 days each). The same number of days is found in 12: 6; and in 13: 5 we have 42 months again. In 12: 14 there is a similar period described as 'three years and a half'; it is literally, as in the R.V., 'a time, and times, and half a time'. All these descriptions therefore refer to a similar length of time, which may conveniently be dealt with here.

The various ways of describing this period go back to the book of Daniel. In Dan. 9: 27 a week is spoken of, and the context makes it clear that this is a week of years, i.e. seven years. This 'week' is divided into two parts, so that we have three and a half years twice over. In Dan. 7: 25 and 12: 7 there is the expression 'a time and times and half a time'; and the period is given in days in 12: 11, actually 1290 days. It is clear that to understand the time references in Revelation we must take Daniel into account.

In the book of Daniel the reference is to the events of the reign of Antiochus IV (Epiphanes), ruler of Syria and the great persecutor of the Jews. A week of years is divided into two halves (9: 27); the middle point corresponds to the action of Antiochus in 168 B.C. in setting up an image of the Greek god Zeus on the altar in Jerusalem. This is what Daniel calls 'the abomination that maketh desolate' or some such expression (11: 31; 12: 11; 9: 27). The phrase 'abomination of desolation' occurs in 1 Macc. 1: 54 where a straightforward account of these events is given.

The author of Daniel, who wrote about 167 B.C. while all this was happening, expected that this desecration would last for three and a half years (12: 11) during which there would be acute persecution, and then divine deliverance would come. It so happened that the Jews did recover possession of their temple in 165 B.C., three years after its defilement, and they have celebrated the event ever since in the feast of Dedication (or Chanukkah). But the glorious New Age with a resurrection of the dead, such as Dan. 12 had forecast, did not begin at that time. The Jews (and later the Christians) therefore took the happenings of this period as *a foreshadowing of the last years of world history*; and it is this belief that can be recognized in Revelation and elsewhere in the New Testament. (In Daniel everything is put in the future tense as though its prophecies were written in the sixth century instead of the second; and so it is easy to take these forecasts as referring to events that still lie in the future.)

This belief, that the events of the time of Antiochus were a foreshadowing of the events of the time of Antichrist, is an important one and is an essential clue to many passages of the New Testament.

Among the events of Antiochus' time were the following six; most of them are put into the form of prophecies in Daniel but in the books of Maccabees they are recorded in historical fashion:

(1) A falling away or apostasy (Dan. 11: 30, 32; 1 Macc. 1: 15).

(2) A great figure of evil opposed to God (Dan. 11: 36-7).

(3) He profanes the temple, setting up the abomination (Dan. 11: 31).

(4) The profanation is the signal for the flight of the faithful to the mountains or the wilderness (1 Macc. 1: 28-9).

(5) A tribulation more severe than any known before (Dan. 12: 1).

(6) The tribulation would last for three and a half years (Dan. 12: 11). This period of time, as we have seen, was the second half of a week of years, this week being the final seven years before the dawn of a new age.

All these reappear in the New Testament as the features which are to herald the return of Christ, and most of them are included in Revelation.

(1) The falling away or apostasy (2 Thess. 2: 3; Mark 13: 6).

(2) 'The man doomed to perdition' or the beast (2 Thess. 2: 3-4; Rev. 11: 7).

(3) The profaning of the temple (2 Thess. 2: 4) and the setting up of 'the abomination of desolation, of which the prophet Daniel spoke, standing in the holy place' (Matt. 24: 15; cf. Mark 13: 14).

(4) The profanation is the signal for the flight of the faithful; 'when you see "the abomination..."' those who are in Judaea must take to the hills' (Mark 13: 14; cf. Rev. 12: 6, 14).

(5) A distress such as had never happened before (Mark 13: 18-19, where the exact terms of Dan. 12: 1 are used; Rev. 7: 14; 12: 12-14).

(6) The time of stress, marked by the supremacy of the beast, is to last for three and a half years (Rev. 13: 5, etc.).

It is this last point which concerns us most at the moment. The three and a half year period in Revelation (in its various forms) usually means the very last years before the end, but not always. We must bear in mind the seven-year period divided into two equal parts; and the prophesying of the two witnesses should probably be allocated to the *first* half of the week of years.

Looked at in this way, the time scheme is quite a simple one; and the various days and months, which at first seem so difficult and baffling, fit into a clear pattern. All we have to remember is a period of seven years divided into two equal parts. The preaching of the two witnesses occupies the first half. The second half is the time of bitter trial when Antichrist reigns supreme, and it is in this period that the fearful events of chapters 13–19 take place. (It may be mentioned that several Christian writers of the early centuries took this line of interpretation, including Victorinus, one of the earliest commentators on Revelation. He lived in the third century. Hippolytus, who lived in the early half of the same century, put the matter clearly when he wrote of a week of years being divided into two parts; half of it, he said, will be taken up by the two prophets of Rev. 11, and during the other half the tyrant Antichrist will reign and persecute the Church.)

The 42 months of Rev. 11: 2 should also probably be placed in the first half of the 'week', thus coinciding with the preaching of the witnesses in verse 3. But all the other references apply to the last three and a half years of world history. *

THE SEVENTH TRUMPET

15 Then the seventh angel blew his trumpet; and voices were heard in heaven shouting:

'The sovereignty of the world has passed to our Lord and his Christ, and he shall reign for ever and ever!'

16 And the twenty-four elders, seated on their thrones before
17 God, fell on their faces and worshipped God, saying:

'We give thee thanks, O Lord God, sovereign over all, who art and who wast, because thou hast taken thy great power into thy hands and entered upon thy reign. The nations raged, but thy day of retribution 18 has come. Now is the time for the dead to be judged; now is the time for recompense to thy servants the prophets, to thy dedicated people, and all who honour thy name, both great and small, the time to destroy those who destroy the earth.'

Then God's temple in heaven was laid open, and 19 within the temple was seen the ark of his covenant. There came flashes of lightning and peals of thunder, an earthquake, and a storm of hail.

✶ This passage is a further example of the author's use of heavenly interludes and his inclusion of hymns and songs. One would expect to find the third woe here, but no mention of it is made. Instead there is this burst of triumph from unspecified voices in heaven and from the twenty-four elders announcing the divine victory. There is a sense in which the seventh trumpet extends over the succeeding chapters (12–19) including the outpouring of the seven bowls with their plagues, so that a good deal of 'woe' is involved indirectly. But at the moment all this is forgotten in the burst of praise. The victory is so sure that it is spoken of as already achieved. We have a saying, 'It's all over bar the shouting'; we mean that the result of some contest is so certain that although it may still last for a time the result is a foregone conclusion. That is the case here, with the difference that the shout of victory has already begun.

15. *our Lord and his Christ.* This is a reminiscence of Ps. 2: 2 which speaks of the Lord and his anointed. The psalm begins with the words, 'Why do the nations rage?' and this phrase is reflected in verse 18.

17–18. F. C. Grant aptly compares this song to a 'hymn of anticipated victory sung by the troops on their way to battle' (*Nelson's Bible Commentary*).

19. Again *God's temple* is revealed; we have previously seen the golden altar, but now *the ark of his covenant* appears. ✻

THE WOMAN ROBED WITH THE SUN

12 Next appeared a great portent in heaven, a woman robed with the sun, beneath her feet the moon, and on her head
2 a crown of twelve stars. She was pregnant, and in the anguish of her labour she cried out to be delivered.
3 Then a second portent appeared in heaven: a great red dragon with seven heads and ten horns; on his heads
4 were seven diadems, and with his tail he swept down a third of the stars in the sky and flung them to the earth. The dragon stood in front of the woman who was about to give birth, so that when her child was born he might
5 devour it. She gave birth to a male child, who is destined to rule all nations with an iron rod. But her child was
6 snatched up to God and his throne; and the woman herself fled into the wilds, where she had a place prepared for her by God, there to be sustained for twelve hundred and sixty days.

✻ It is generally thought that a pagan story provides the imagery of this section. Several ancient myths (Egyptian, Babylonian, etc.) describe a monster who waits to devour a child about to be born; the child is nevertheless safely born and escapes; in some cases he destroys the monster. The story was current in the area where John lived. There is no difficulty in supposing that he adapted parts of this myth to Christian use, for dreams and visions are often built up from materials which already exist in the mind. Greek legends concerning the birth of Apollo said that his mother Leto was pursued by the serpent Python when she was pregnant. Python knew that he was fated to be slain by Leto's son. The sea-god Poseidon, however, came to Leto's help and conveyed her to the island of Delos, where she safely gave birth to Apollo. It is an interesting point that the island of Delos was visible to John from Patmos and this may help to explain his use of this story which he has modified and adapted to his own purpose.

The woman stands for Israel, the people of God, from whom Jesus sprang, as far as his natural descent was concerned (Rom. 9: 5). The language of the second verse reflects Isa. 66: 7 where Zion is described as a woman in travail. The child is of course Jesus, as the language of verse 5 clearly shows.

1. *a crown of twelve stars* should be taken as a reference to the twelve tribes of Israel.

3. *a great red dragon* stands for the devil (or Satan). His seven heads and ten horns are also characteristics of the beast of the following chapter and can best be explained in connexion with the beast; see the note on 13: 1. In the Old Testament Satan is nowhere called a dragon, but there are a number of references to a sea-monster, sometimes named Rahab. According to Babylonian legend, there was a great struggle at the beginning of time between Marduk, the god of light, and Tiamat the sea-monster, who stood for chaos. Marduk mastered Tiamat and the latter was imprisoned in the depths of the sea. It is this myth which stands behind a number of the Old Testament references to the dragon. After the close of the Old Testament period the conception of Satan was greatly expanded; see the note below on verse 7. In this chapter he is identified with the primeval dragon and also (verse 9) with the serpent of Gen. 3.

5. The life and ministry of Jesus are passed over in silence and we pass from Bethlehem to the Ascension.

to rule all nations with an iron rod. The words come from

Ps. 2: 9; we have met them before in 2: 27 and they occur again in 19: 15.

6. The woman is still to be understood as Israel but in the more restricted sense of the Jewish Christian Church. Her flight *into the wilds...for twelve hundred and sixty days* stands for the preservation of the Jewish Christians during the 3½ years of Antichrist's persecution. Early commentators like Victorinus (third century) connect this verse with Mark 13: 14–20 which bids 'those who are in Judaea' to 'take to the hills' as the great tribulation begins.

A long period is thus telescoped in this section (verses 1–6); we pass from the birth of Jesus to his Ascension, and then on to the final tribulation. But the point of it all is to show that behind the persecution which the readers are enduring, a persecution which is soon to burst upon them in its full fury, there is the continuing hostility of the devil. Jesus himself was endangered by the same forces which are arrayed against them. There is nothing strange about their plight. 'As they persecuted me, they will persecute you; they will follow your teaching as little as they have followed mine. It is on my account that they will treat you thus...' (John 15: 20–1). ✳

THE DEFEAT OF THE DRAGON

7 Then war broke out in heaven. Michael and his angels waged war upon the dragon. The dragon and his angels
8 fought, but they had not the strength to win, and no
9 foothold was left them in heaven. So the great dragon was thrown down, that serpent of old that led the whole world astray, whose name is Satan, or the Devil—thrown down to the earth, and his angels with him.

10   Then I heard a voice in heaven proclaiming aloud: 'This is the hour of victory for our God, the hour of his sovereignty and power, when his Christ comes to his

rightful rule! For the accuser of our brothers is over-
thrown, who day and night accused them before our
God. By the sacrifice of the Lamb they have conquered 11
him, and by the testimony which they uttered; for they
did not hold their lives too dear to lay them down.
Rejoice then, you heavens and you that dwell in them! 12
But woe to you, earth and sea, for the Devil has come
down to you in great fury, knowing that his time is short!'

When the dragon found that he had been thrown down 13
to the earth, he went in pursuit of the woman who had
given birth to the male child. But the woman was given 14
two great eagle's wings, to fly to the place in the wilds
where for three years and a half she was to be sustained,
out of reach of the serpent. From his mouth the serpent 15
spewed a flood of water after the woman to sweep her
away with its spate. But the earth came to her rescue 16
and opened its mouth and swallowed the river which the
dragon spewed from his mouth. At this the dragon grew 17
furious with the woman, and went off to wage war on the
rest of her offspring, that is, on those who keep God's
commandments and maintain their testimony to Jesus.
He took his stand on the sea-shore.   **13**

✳ The scene now changes to heaven. The devil is defeated by
Michael and is cast down to the earth. He knows that but a
little time remains before his final arrest—the $3\frac{1}{2}$ years
mentioned in verse 14. He therefore does as much damage as
he can. The purpose of this section is to show that the devil
is a vanquished enemy; he is still permitted to inflict great
sufferings on the servants of Christ, but these activities are the
final convulsions of a conquered foe.

He is again seen pursuing 'the woman', the Jewish
Christians who are enabled to escape him (verse 14). The

full force of his attack then falls on *the rest of her offspring* (verse 17) evidently the Gentile Christians. (Even Gentile Christians are the offspring of the Israel of God.) This interpretation agrees with chapter 7 where the Jewish Christians are 'sealed' while the Gentile Christians 'from every nation' bear the full impact of 'the great ordeal'.

It will be seen that verse 14 is virtually a repetition of verse 6; both describe the woman finding refuge in the wilds for 1260 days or 3½ years. 12: 1–6 is an advance along the *horizontal* plane of history and it reaches its climax in this final period of 3½ years; this advance may be illustrated by means of a horizontal line ——. 12: 7–14 deals with the *vertical* conception of heaven and earth; it does not take us back in time but upwards in space, into the heavenly realm; its climax comes with the fall of Satan to the earth, which begins the same 3½ year period. This may be indicated by a dropped perpendicular |. Verses 6 and 14 mark the same point of time, where the horizontal and the vertical meet ⌐. From this point the story proceeds as a single whole.

In verses 1–6 John has told his readers: this persecution you are enduring is but a part of a long struggle; your Lord had to face the same diabolical opposition even from the time of his birth. In verses 7–17 he is saying: the devil is a beaten foe; his fury springs from the fact that he knows *his time is short* (verse 12). Hold fast to the end of this grim period.

7. It is at first surprising that the devil should be found in heaven, and that his opponent should be Michael. It must be remembered that in the Old Testament Satan, while freely roving the earth, has access to God's presence (Job 1–2; Zech. 3) and almost plays the part of public prosecutor as though he held an essential place in the divine ordering of the universe. But by New Testament times he has become a figure of evil and the great opponent of God. Nevertheless, traces of the old conception still linger and in this very chapter he is described as *the accuser of our brothers...who day and night accused them before our God* (verse 10). This helps to explain his

presence in heaven. But now war is waged upon him and he is finally cast out. John apparently regards this expulsion as taking place just at the beginning of the final tribulation. For other conceptions of the casting down of Satan see Luke 10: 18 (which connects it with the success of the seventy-two disciples in casting out demons) and John 12: 31 (which connects it with the cross).

Michael was one of the seven archangels (see 8: 2 and note). His vital place in the present story is to be explained by Dan. ´12: 1 where the description of the unprecedented tribulation is introduced with the words, 'And at that time shall Michael stand up, the great prince which standeth for the children of thy people'. The unspecified exploit of Michael is explained by John as the defeat of the devil. It should be noted that, in Daniel, behind the various nations stand angelic powers and there are hints of struggle in the supernatural realm between these powers; see especially 10: 13, 'But the prince [i.e. angel] of the kingdom of Persia withstood me... but, lo, Michael, one of the chief princes, came to help me'. The suffering Church of John's day is reminded that its conflicts on earth reflect a superhuman contest in heaven.

9. The various names of Satan are interesting. He is (*a*) *the great red dragon*; cf. verse 3; (*b*) *that serpent of old*, for Jewish thought had come to connect the serpent of Gen. 3 with the evil one; (*c*) *Satan*, which means adversary; and (*d*) *the Devil*, literally slanderer; this connects with the description in verse 10, *the accuser*.

10–12. Another example of the way in which Christian song is interspersed throughout the book. In the midst of her anguish the Church hears the heavenly song of victory.

11. The suggestion of the passage is that the accusations of the devil are false, for he is a slanderer. But even if they were true, he could be overcome *by the sacrifice* (literally 'blood') *of the Lamb*, the Lamb 'who takes away the sin of the world' (John 1: 29). See 5: 9 and note.

14. It was 'on eagles' wings' that Israel escaped from

Egypt (Exod. 19: 4). The same imagery is used here to describe this new deliverance.

the wilds. As mentioned above this should probably be connected with Mark 13: 14–20 and the injunction to those in Judaea to fly to the wilderness as the final tribulation begins, just as they did in the days of Antiochus (see the note on 'the three and a half years' under chapter 11).

15–16. The *flood of water* is swallowed by the ground. This may simply be a part of the story which John is using, a picturesque detail without any particular Christian application.

17. *the rest of her offspring*: probably the Gentile Christians who in the wider field of the Roman world were to bear the main brunt of the attack.

The central character of this chapter has been the dragon; the main character of the next (ch. 13) will be the beast. Just as the early judgements of the book are introduced by visions of God the Father (ch. 4) and the Lamb (ch. 5), so the latter half of the book is introduced by these two chapters presenting their hellish counterparts, the dragon and the beast. ✻

THE BEAST FROM THE SEA

Then out of the sea I saw a beast rising. It had ten horns and seven heads. On its horns were ten diadems, and on
2 each head a blasphemous name. The beast I saw was like a leopard, but its feet were like a bear's and its mouth like a lion's mouth. The dragon conferred upon it his power
3 and rule, and great authority. One of its heads appeared to have received a death-blow; but the mortal wound was healed. The whole world went after the beast in
4 wondering admiration. Men worshipped the dragon because he had conferred his authority upon the beast; they worshipped the beast also, and chanted, 'Who is like the Beast? Who can fight against it?'

The beast was allowed to mouth bombast and blas- 5
phemy, and was given the right to reign for forty-two
months. It opened its mouth in blasphemy against God, 6
reviling his name and his heavenly dwelling. It was also 7
allowed to wage war on God's people and to defeat them,
and was granted authority over every tribe and people,
language and nation. All on earth will worship it, 8
except those whose names the Lamb that was slain keeps
in his roll of the living, written there since the world
was made.

Hear, you who have ears to hear! Whoever is meant 9, 10
for prison, to prison he goes. Whoever takes the sword
to kill, by the sword he is bound to be killed. Here the
fortitude and faithfulness of God's people have their
place.

✶ The beast, which made a brief appearance in 11: 7, is now
fully described in all its frightfulness. It represents the persecuting Roman empire concentrated in Nero, who was
expected to return to the earth. The imagery comes from
Dan. 7 where the empires of Babylon, the Medes, Persia
and Greece are represented by four grisly beasts. What was
said in the opening pages about Nero needs particularly to be
remembered in connexion with this chapter. Further details
about the beast are given in chapter 17 and these throw light
on the present passage. As in Dan. 7, the king and the kingdom
tend to be identified; at first the monster is the Roman empire
but as the chapter develops it comes to stand for a single ruler
with supernatural powers and with a deadly hate against the
servants of God.

1. *out of the sea*. In Dan. 7 the four beasts 'came up from
the sea'. The *seven heads* stand for seven kings, as stated in
17: 9–10. It has been suggested that the number seven was
reached by adding together the heads of the four beasts of

79

Dan. 7; the leopard had four heads; the lion, the bear and the fourth beast had one each—total seven. But a seven-headed monster was known to ancient mythology in Palestine and elsewhere.

The *ten horns* no doubt come from Dan. 7: 7 where they represent ten kings. But in Revelation, as we have seen, it is the seven heads which stand for kings. However, the ten horns are not merely a piece of imagery taken over without special meaning (though this may be the case with the ten horns of the dragon in 12: 3). They are given a meaning in 17: 12 where they appear to stand for ten Parthian rulers who advance with Nero against Rome somewhat along the lines of popular expectation.

a blasphemous name. This refers to the divine honours claimed for themselves by the emperors.

2. This recalls the leopard, bear and lion of Dan. 7: 4–6. *The dragon* is the devil, who works through his instrument, the beast.

3. This is an important verse for the interpretation of the whole book. Two points need to be made here. (*a*) The verse refers undoubtedly to the belief that Nero was not finally removed from his baneful work on earth; he would return: *the mortal wound was healed.* The same idea is repeated in 17: 8: 'he who once was alive, and is alive no longer, but has yet to ascend...'. (*b*) There is a parallel with what is said of the Lamb. Jesus also was dead and came to life again (1: 18); his work on earth is unfinished. The parallel is clearer in the Greek, for the same expression is used both of the Lamb and the beast. The similarity can be seen in the R.V.; thus in 5: 6 we have the words 'a Lamb standing, as though it had been slain', and in 13: 3 'as though it had been smitten unto death'. The same Greek verb is used for 'slain' and 'smitten'; it occurs again in 13: 8: *the Lamb that was slain.*

5. *bombast,* i.e. boastful words.

The *forty-two months* are to be taken literally; it was believed that Antichrist would reign for $3\frac{1}{2}$ years. This tradition persisted and it is mentioned by Augustine in his *City of God* (20: 23).

7. Just as Nero was the great persecutor of the Christians at Rome in the period following the fire of A.D. 64, so at his reappearance he is to wage a violent persecution on *God's people*. He is allowed to have *authority over every tribe and people, language and nation*. In this he is again a replica of Jesus, the same four words being used in the song of praise to the Lamb, who purchased for God 'men of every tribe and language, people and nation' (5: 9).

8. Grammatically the words *since the world was made* could be taken either with *the Lamb that was slain*, or (as in the N.E.B.) with the word *written*. Those who prefer the former point to the fact that the sacrifice of Christ was not only an event in history; it also revealed God's continual suffering over man's sin from the beginning. The idea of names being written in a book is found in the Old Testament; for example, Moses prayed that the sin of the people might be forgiven even if it meant the erasure of his own name from God's book (Exod. 32: 32).

9–10. This section closes with another call to *fortitude and faithfulness*. The words are ambiguous, but they may mean that the Christians are not to strike a blow in their own defence—as Peter did in Gethsemane when he provoked the words of Jesus which seem to be echoed here, 'Put up your sword. All who take the sword die by the sword' (Matt. 26: 52). ✻

THE SECOND BEAST

Then I saw another beast, which came up out of the earth; 11 it had two horns like a lamb's, but spoke like a dragon. It wielded all the authority of the first beast in its presence, 12 and made the earth and its inhabitants worship this first beast, whose mortal wound had been healed. It worked 13 great miracles, even making fire come down from heaven

14 to earth before men's eyes. By the miracles it was
allowed to perform in the presence of the beast it deluded
the inhabitants of the earth, and made them erect an
image in honour of the beast that had been wounded by
15 the sword and yet lived. It was allowed to give breath
to the image of the beast, so that it could speak, and
could cause all who would not worship the image to be
16 put to death. Moreover, it caused everyone, great and
small, rich and poor, slave and free, to be branded with
17 a mark on his right hand or forehead, and no one was
allowed to buy or sell unless he bore this beast's mark,
18 either name or number. (Here is the key; and anyone
who has intelligence may work out the number of the
beast. The number represents a man's name, and the
numerical value of its letters is six hundred and sixty-six.)

✶ The second beast is rather a mysterious figure. In 19: 20
he is called 'the false prophet'. The most likely interpretation
sees in him a representative of the pagan priesthood associated
with emperor-worship. This would suit perfectly what is
said in verse 12 and the sequel; the second beast fosters the
worship of the first.

12. Further traces of the belief in Nero's return may be
seen in the words about the *first beast, whose mortal wound had
been healed,* and in the closing words of verse 14 *the beast that
had been wounded by the sword and yet lived.*

14. *made them erect an image.* To such lengths was emperor-
worship carried. One is reminded of the similar situation in
Dan. 3 and Nebuchadnezzar's image of gold which all his
subjects were to worship.

16. The mark on the hand or the forehead provides another
piece of parallelism; just as the Lamb's followers had a name
'written on their foreheads' (cf. 14: 1) so the beast's worshippers
are marked in a similar way.

18. The most widely accepted interpretation is that this number stands for 'Nero Caesar'. If these two names are written in Hebrew the numerical value comes to 666. Any name may be turned into a number by taking the first letter of the alphabet for 1, the second for 2 and so on; then when you have reached 10 the next letters become 20, 30, etc.; and after 100 the other hundreds follow. The number 666 alone would be far from conclusive in indicating Nero, but strong support is given by the fact that so many other factors in these chapters point to him. ✻

Visions of the End

THE LAMB AND THE THREE ANGELS

THEN I LOOKED, and on Mount Zion stood the Lamb, **14** and with him were a hundred and forty-four thousand who had his name and the name of his Father written on their foreheads. I heard a sound from heaven 2 like the noise of rushing water and the deep roar of thunder; it was the sound of harpers playing on their harps. There before the throne, and the four living 3 creatures and the elders, they were singing a new song. That song no one could learn except the hundred and forty-four thousand, who alone from the whole world had been ransomed. These are men who did not defile 4 themselves with women, for they have kept themselves chaste, and they follow the Lamb wherever he goes. They have been ransomed as the firstfruits of humanity for God and the Lamb. No lie was found in their lips; they 5 are faultless.

6   Then I saw an angel flying in mid-heaven, with an
eternal gospel to proclaim to those on earth, to every
7 nation and tribe, language and people. He cried in a
loud voice, 'Fear God and pay him homage; for the hour
of his judgement has come! Worship him who made
heaven and earth, the sea and the water-springs!'

8   Then another angel, a second, followed, and he cried,
'Fallen, fallen is Babylon the great, she who has made
all nations drink the fierce wine of her fornication!'

9   Yet a third angel followed, crying out loud, 'Whoever
worships the beast and its image and receives its mark on
10 his forehead or hand, he shall drink the wine of God's
wrath, poured undiluted into the cup of his vengeance.
He shall be tormented in sulphurous flames before the
11 holy angels and before the Lamb. The smoke of their
torment will rise for ever and ever, and there will be no
respite day or night for those who worship the beast
12 and its image or receive the mark of its name.' Here the
fortitude of God's people has its place—in keeping God's
commands and remaining loyal to Jesus.

13   Moreover, I heard a voice from heaven, saying, 'Write
this: "Happy are the dead who die in the faith of Christ!
Henceforth", says the Spirit, "they may rest from their
labours; for they take with them the record of their
deeds."'

* 1-5. One of the features of this book is the writer's habit
of interspersing among his visions of doom glimpses of the
final bliss of the servants of God. His messages of punishment
and tribulation are thus relieved by the quieter music of these
interludes; and though they are strictly out of chronological
sequence they serve a purpose in keeping before us the

ultimate bliss and peace which will remain when the violent storms have dispersed. It is in this light that we should regard the present paragraph.

1. *Mount Zion* should here be regarded as the heavenly not the earthly Zion. In Heb. 12: 22 Mount Zion is identified with the heavenly Jerusalem with its myriads of angels.

Are we to identify the *hundred and forty-four thousand* spoken of here with the group similarly numbered in 7: 4-8? Probably not. The people mentioned in 7: 4-8 are from the twelve tribes of Israel; in the present passage the company consists of those *who alone from the whole world had been ransomed* (verse 3). Moreover they are described as celibates (i.e. unmarried) (verse 4) and this would seem to mark them out from the earlier group which is not described in the same way.

4. This verse is problematical. In the New Testament generally sexual relations (which are of course restricted to husband and wife) are not spoken of as in themselves defiling. The reference to *men who did not defile themselves with women* seems to be inappropriate language. We can only conclude that the reference is to men vowed to celibacy; for them marriage would be defiling for it would involve the breaking of their vow. The words of Matt. 19: 12 may be recalled: 'there are others who have themselves renounced marriage for the sake of the kingdom of Heaven. Let those accept it who can.' Some prefer to interpret the language of 14: 4 in a symbolic way; cf. 2 Cor. 11: 2 where Paul says to the Corinthians, 'I betrothed you to Christ, thinking to present you as a chaste virgin to her true and only husband'.

The group in question does not stand for the whole Church but is described as *the firstfruits of humanity*; the main body of the redeemed will appear later.

6-12. Three angels are seen in turn, each one making an important declaration.

6-7. *an eternal Gospel.* 'Gospel' usually means good news, but here it is a message of impending doom. It is a gospel in the sense that it includes a call to repentance (verse 7), and it is eternal because lasting in its effects. It is concerned not with temporary measures but with final judgement.

8. The second angel sees in anticipation the fall of *Babylon the great* (Rome); the actual incident is described in the graphic words of chapter 18.

9–12. The *third angel* issues a stern warning against compromise. Those who in fear of man worship the emperor or his image are reminded that it would be more fitting to fear God, who alone has supreme power over men's destiny (cf. Luke 12: 4–5). It should be frankly admitted that the thought in verse 11 is sub-Christian. The stress of the time when the book was written helps to explain it; but it is impossible to reconcile with the teaching of Jesus the statement here made that those who have fallen into the sin of emperor-worship will be tormented day and night for ever. No possible purpose could be served by keeping in existence the victims of continual suffering without offering them any prospect of release.

13. In contrast to the threats of 9–12 there is a promise of happiness for those who remain steadfast. *

THE HARVEST AND THE VINTAGE

14 Then as I looked there appeared a white cloud, and on the cloud sat one like a son of man. He had on his head a
15 crown of gold and in his hand a sharp sickle. Another angel came out of the temple and called in a loud voice to him who sat on the cloud: 'Stretch out your sickle and reap; for harvest-time has come, and earth's crop is
16 over-ripe.' So he who sat on the cloud put his sickle to the earth and its harvest was reaped.

17 Then another angel came out of the heavenly temple,
18 and he also had a sharp sickle. Then from the altar came yet another, the angel who has authority over fire, and he

shouted to the one with the sharp sickle: 'Stretch out your sickle, and gather in earth's grape-harvest, for its clusters are ripe.' So the angel put his sickle to the earth 19 and gathered in its grapes, and threw them into the great winepress of God's wrath. The winepress was trodden 20 outside the city, and for two hundred miles around blood flowed from the press to the height of the horses' bridles.

✻ Further angels appear at this point with announcements of the rapidly approaching doom.

14. It is probable that the *one like a son of man* is to be understood as an angel. The words are similar to the phrase of Dan. 7: 13, a source of Jesus' self-designation 'the Son of Man'. But similar expressions in Dan. 8: 16; 10: 16, 18, appear to refer to angels.

15–16. The imagery of the *harvest* is derived from the Old Testament. The judgement which Joel foretold is expressed in these terms. 'Put ye in the sickle, for the harvest is ripe' (Joel 3: 13).

17–20. The imagery of the *grape-harvest* is also based upon an Old Testament passage, Isa. 63: 1–6, the influence of which appears again in Rev. 19: 15. Instead of grape-juice there is human blood, flowing so deep that it seems to reach the bridles of the horses. Cf. Enoch 100: 3, 'And the horse shall walk up to the breast in the blood of sinners, and the chariot shall be submerged to its height'.

This brings us to the end of four difficult chapters, 11–14, which have had the effect of slowing up the action of the book. They have, however, served a number of useful purposes at the mid-point of the story. Among other things, they have given us close-ups, as it were, of the beast and the Lamb, the two contestants for world supremacy. From this point the drama moves swiftly to its climax. In chapters 15 and 16 there are the seven bowls, and then in 17–19 the final destruction of Babylon and the beast. ✻

THE SONG OF VICTORY AND THE SEVEN ANGELS

15 Then I saw another great and astonishing portent in heaven: seven angels with seven plagues, the last plagues of all, for with them the wrath of God is consummated.

2   I saw what seemed a sea of glass shot with fire, and beside the sea of glass, holding the harps which God had given them, were those who had won the victory over the beast and its image and the number of its name.

3   They were singing the song of Moses, the servant of God, and the song of the Lamb, as they chanted:

'Great and marvellous are thy deeds, O Lord God, sovereign over all; just and true are thy ways, thou
4 king of the ages. Who shall not revere thee, Lord, and do homage to thy name? For thou alone art holy. All nations shall come and worship in thy presence, for thy just dealings stand revealed.'

5   After this, as I looked, the sanctuary of the heavenly
6 Tent of Testimony was thrown open, and out of it came the seven angels with the seven plagues. They were robed in fine linen, clean and shining, and had golden girdles
7 round their breasts. Then one of the four living creatures gave the seven angels seven golden bowls full of the
8 wrath of God who lives for ever and ever; and the sanctuary was filled with smoke from the glory of God and his power, so that no one could enter it until the seven plagues of the seven angels were completed.

✶ Earlier parts of Revelation have been taken up with the seven seals and the seven trumpets; now begins the record of the seven plagues. The present chapter is an introduction and it brings in the seven angels who bear the *bowls full of the wrath of God*. After the opening announcement of verse 1, there intervenes a short section (verses 2-4) describing the worship maintained in heaven. A similar emphasis upon celestial worship, in chapters 4-5, preceded the opening of the seven seals.

2. *the sea of glass* appears as in 4: 6. The phrase *shot with fire* may be an attempt to describe the sparkling of its crystal radiance. The triumph song is sung by *those who had won the victory over the beast*. In what sense were they victorious? They were probably martyred and thus seemed defeated; but they were nevertheless the victors in that they had not succumbed to all the efforts and threats put forward to make them give up their faith. One is reminded of the death of Jesus, which looked like defeat but was in reality a great victory (John 12: 31-2).

3. Running through many parts of the New Testament is the thought of the Christian deliverance as a new Exodus. In old time God had rescued the people of Israel from Egypt; so through Christ a new deliverance, on the spiritual level, had been achieved. There was a new Passover (1 Cor. 5: 7), a new covenant (1 Cor. 11: 25; 2 Cor. 3: 6), a new wilderness period (1 Cor. 10: 1-11); and in a sense Moses gives place to Jesus. The Jewish people came to think of Moses as 'the first deliverer' and the Messiah, whom they expected, as 'the second deliverer'. This background helps us to understand the language of this verse. *The song of Moses...and the song of the Lamb* are virtually the same song, celebrating divine deliverance. After the Exodus came the triumphant paean of Moses recorded in Exod. 15. The words given here in Rev. 15: 3-4 would be equally appropriate to the old Exodus and the new; in both events the same delivering mercy was revealed. There may be a hint too that the victory over Pharaoh (so prominent in Exod. 15) foreshadowed the victory over the beast. The triumph song in Exod. 15 was sung by the shores

of the Red Sea; this new song is also sung by a sea, the heavenly sea of verse 2.

5. The heavenly sanctuary is here described in terms of the Tent of Testimony, the precursor of the temple. When the Tent was completed it was filled with the glory of the Lord (Exod. 40: 34). So it is with the sanctuary in heaven. The further idea of smoke recalls Isa. 6: 4, 'the house was filled with smoke'. ✳

THE SEVEN BOWLS OF WRATH

16 Then from the sanctuary I heard a loud voice, and it said to the seven angels, 'Go and pour out the seven bowls of God's wrath on the earth.'

2 So the first angel went and poured his bowl on the earth; and foul malignant sores appeared on those men that wore the mark of the beast and worshipped its image.

3 The second angel poured his bowl on the sea, and it turned to blood like the blood from a corpse; and every living thing in the sea died.

4 The third angel poured his bowl on the rivers and springs, and they turned to blood.

5 Then I heard the angel of the waters say, 'Just art thou in these thy judgements, thou Holy One who art and 6 wast; for they shed the blood of thy people and of thy prophets, and thou hast given them blood to drink. They 7 have their deserts!' And I heard the altar cry, 'Yes, Lord God, sovereign over all, true and just are thy judgements!'

8 The fourth angel poured his bowl on the sun; and it 9 was allowed to burn men with its flames. They were

fearfully burned; but they only cursed the name of God who had the power to inflict such plagues, and they refused to repent or do him homage.

The fifth angel poured his bowl on the throne of the 10 beast; and its kingdom was plunged in darkness. Men gnawed their tongues in agony, but they only cursed 11 the God of heaven for their pains and sores, and would not repent of what they had done.

The sixth angel poured his bowl on the great river 12 Euphrates; and its water was dried up, to prepare the way for the kings from the east.

Then I saw coming from the mouth of the dragon, 13 the mouth of the beast, and the mouth of the false prophet, three foul spirits like frogs. These spirits were devils, 14 with power to work miracles. They were sent out to muster all the kings of the world for the great day of battle of God the sovereign Lord. ('That is the day when 15 I come like a thief! Happy the man who stays awake and keeps on his clothes, so that he will not have to go naked and ashamed for all to see!') So they assembled 16 the kings at the place called in Hebrew Armageddon.

Then the seventh angel poured his bowl on the air; 17 and out of the sanctuary came a loud voice from the throne, which said, 'It is over!' And there followed 18 flashes of lightning and peals of thunder, and a violent earthquake, like none before it in human history, so violent it was. The great city was split in three; the cities 19 of the world fell in ruin; and God did not forget Babylon the great, but made her drink the cup which was filled with the fierce wine of his vengeance. Every island 20 vanished; there was not a mountain to be seen. Huge 21 hailstones, weighing perhaps a hundredweight, fell on men from the sky; and they cursed God for the plague of hail, because that plague was so severe.

✳ Seven plagues are produced by the pouring out of the seven bowls; and these are somewhat similar to the plagues inflicted on the Egyptians. In this way there is a continuation of the reminiscences of the Exodus which we found in the previous chapter. The ten plagues, however, have to be accommodated to the seven-fold scheme which controls the whole book.

2. The *sores* correspond to the plague of boils in Exod. 9: 10–11.

3–6. The turning of the waters to blood answers to a similar plague described in Exod. 7: 17–21. A grim appropriateness is seen in this plague; the people who have shed so much Christian blood deserve to have their drinking water changed to the same fluid. *They have their deserts!* (verse 6).

7. The speaking altar is difficult to understand. Some light is thrown on it by the fact that the souls of the martyrs were, in 6: 9–10, described as being 'underneath the altar' or at its foot.

8–12. The fourth to the sixth bowls do not at first sight correspond to Egyptian plagues; but the fifth plague results in the beast's kingdom being *plunged in darkness* and this may connect with the plague of darkness in Exod. 10: 21–3.

10. *the throne of the beast*: Rome.

12. The drying up of the *river Euphrates* recalls the drying up of the sea in Exod. 14: 21, though this of course was not one of the ten plagues but was to enable the people of Israel to escape. Here, however, the reference is probably connected with the expected return of Nero from the east. (Incidentally this is not inconsistent with his return from the abyss, 11: 7.) The Sibylline Oracles speak of Nero returning from 'beyond the ford of Euphrates...lifting up a mighty sword and crossing the Euphrates with many tens of thousands' (4: 115–39). It was believed that he would advance on Rome and

take vengeance for its rejection of him. In the twenty years
after Nero's death three pretenders appeared, calling themselves Nero. One of them, named Terentius Maximus,
collected a following in the east and moved towards the
Euphrates; the Parthian king welcomed this alleged Nero and
plotted to use him in an attack on Rome and to reinstate him
on the throne.

the kings from the east. These may well be Parthian satraps
(regional rulers).

13–16. Three frog-like devils incite the kings of the earth
to gather at Armageddon in readiness for the final conflict.

13. The dragon, the beast and the false prophet form a
trinity of evil. The prophet is evidently to be identified with
the second beast of 13: 11–18. The dragon (devil) stands
over against God the Father; the beast against the Son of God;
and the false prophet could be taken as a counterpart of the
Holy Spirit who inspires the true prophets.

14. *all the kings of the world.* These are not the same as 'the
kings from the east' in verse 12. Two strands need to be
distinguished here:

(*a*) There is the tradition that when Nero returned he
would lead the Parthians against Rome. This seems to lie
behind verse 12 where the drying up of the Euphrates enables
'the kings from the east' to advance. In the following chapter
the onslaught of the beast and his allies against Rome is
described (17: 15–18); they plan to burn the city and the great
fire provides the theme of chapter 18.

(*b*) An older tradition envisaged a final battle when the
nations would be arrayed against God (Joel 3: 2; Zeph. 3: 8).
This sometimes took the form of a siege of Jerusalem as in
Zech. 14. Psalm 2 (which Revelation quotes several times)
speaks of the kings of the earth being assembled against God
and his anointed. This appears to be reflected in Rev. 16: 14
where *all the kings of the world* are assembled for God's *great
day of battle*; they assembled at Armageddon (verse 16) but
the battle itself does not take place until 19: 19–21.

The beast plays a leading part in both these enterprises. In 17: 16–18 he is at the head of the ten kings (no doubt *the kings from the east* of 16: 12) who help to destroy Rome; and in 19: 19–21 it is he who leads 'the kings of the earth' in the final battle against the Messiah.

In 16: 12–16 these two strands lie side by side. As Moffatt puts it, 'The fierce invasion of *the kings of the east* seems to give an impulse to *the kings of the world*'. (*Expositor's Greek Testament*.)

16. The word *Armageddon* has not been satisfactorily explained. It is obviously connected with Megiddo, mentioned a number of times in the Old Testament in connexion with battles. Mountains run down from mount Carmel in a south-easterly direction and to the east of these lies the plain of Esdraelon. Megiddo was in the western area of this plain. Kings fought near Megiddo in the olden time (Judg. 5: 19). It was here that Josiah was defeated by Pharaoh (2 Kings 23: 29–30). The death of Josiah was lamented by his people and it may be that the mourning 'in the valley of Megiddon' mentioned in Zech. 12: 11 has some connexion with this tragedy. It will be noticed that the quotation just cited speaks of the 'valley' of Megiddon. But the word Armageddon means mountain of Megiddo. This probably means the hill country near Megiddo.

17–21. The seventh bowl is described at greater length and involves judgements of a wide-ranging kind. The seven bowls and their plagues have some kind of correspondence to the seven trumpets of chapters 8–11. The second in each series turns the sea to blood; with the third in each series the rivers and fountains are turned to blood. The Euphrates appears in the sixth item of each series, and the seventh in both cases brings lightnings, voices, thunders, earthquake and hail.

19. *The great city*: no doubt Rome. The cup *filled with the fierce wine* of divine vengeance is an Old Testament expression; see Jer. 25: 15, where God says, 'Take the cup of the wine of this fury at my hand'. ✳

94

THE GREAT WHORE

Then one of the seven angels that held the seven bowls **17**
came and spoke to me and said, 'Come, and I will show
you the judgement on the great whore, enthroned above
the ocean. The kings of the earth have committed 2
fornication with her, and on the wine of her fornication
men all over the world have made themselves drunk.'
In the Spirit he carried me away into the wilds, and there 3
I saw a woman mounted on a scarlet beast which was
covered with blasphemous names and had seven heads
and ten horns. The woman was clothed in purple and 4
scarlet and bedizened with gold and jewels and pearls.
In her hand she held a gold cup, full of obscenities and
the foulness of her fornication; and written on her fore- 5
head was a name with a secret meaning: 'Babylon the
great, the mother of whores and of every obscenity on
earth.' The woman, I saw, was drunk with the blood of 6
God's people and with the blood of those who had
borne their testimony to Jesus.

✻ A new piece of imagery is introduced here and again it is
to the Old Testament that we must look for its origin. The
relation of Israel to God is sometimes spoken of in terms of
marriage (see especially Hosea) and when Israel turns away
to idols this is a kind of spiritual adultery. The nation is then
spoken of as a harlot; cf. Ezek. 16: 15. Gentile nations are not
usually thought of as sharing in as close a relationship with
God as Israel. And yet the term harlot is at times applied to
them. The idea here is that as a harlot brings ruin and uncleanness on a wide scale so certain nations, through their
spirit of gain and profit-making, had corrupted the surrounding peoples. A good example of this is the case of Tyre; she

had spread a baneful influence in the world and divine judgement would leave her desolate: 'Take an harp, go about the city, thou harlot that hast been forgotten' (Isa. 23: 16). Nahum speaks of Nineveh in similar terms (3: 4). The book of Revelation personifies the city of Rome as *the great whore* (17: 1), a woman *clothed in purple and scarlet* (verse 4).

It may be asked why this additional figure of the harlot is needed; is not the power of Rome already symbolized by the beast? The answer to this is that the woman stands for the *city* of Rome. Popular belief expected Nero to return from the east supported by the Parthians; and he would destroy the city of Rome. In terms of chapter 17 the beast destroys the whore (verse 16). She is a counterpart to the bride of 19: 7; 21: 2 and 9, who is identified with the new Jerusalem. We thus have a symmetrical pattern; on the one hand is the beast, with the whore representing the city of Rome (Babylon), and on the other is the Lamb, with his bride representing the new Jerusalem.

1. *enthroned above the ocean*. Babylon of old was described by Jeremiah as dwelling upon many waters (51: 13), and the description is transferred to the new Babylon (Rome).

3. The whore is first seen as a gorgeously arrayed reveller riding on the beast (to be understood here in the wider sense of the imperial power). Later the beast as Antichrist turns against the whore and destroys her (verse 16). For the *heads* and the *horns* see verses 10–12 and notes.

4. These obscene fornications probably stand for various forms of idolatry rampant among the pagans and more particularly for emperor-worship.

6. Not only was Rome idolatrous and intoxicated with wealth and luxury, it was also the cause of bloodshed, *drunk with the blood of God's people*. It is possible that the bulk of this chapter (which has so little that is specifically Christian) was originally a Jewish document; and the reference here was to the savage punishment meted out to the Jews in the war of 66–70; the addition of the phrase *and with the blood of those*

who had borne their testimony to Jesus gave a Christian application to the oracle. ✳

THE BEAST DESTROYS THE WHORE

As I looked at her I was greatly astonished. But the angel 7
said to me, 'Why are you so astonished? I will tell you
the secret of the woman and of the beast she rides, with
the seven heads and the ten horns. The beast you have 8
seen is he who once was alive, and is alive no longer,
but has yet to ascend out of the abyss before going to
perdition. Those on earth whose names have not been
inscribed in the roll of the living ever since the world
was made will all be astonished to see the beast; for he
once was alive, and is alive no longer, and has still to
appear.

'But here is the clue for those who can interpret it. The 9
seven heads are seven hills on which the woman sits.
They represent also seven kings, of whom five have 10
already fallen, one is now reigning, and the other has yet
to come; and when he does come he is only to last for a
little while. As for the beast that once was alive and is 11
alive no longer, he is an eighth—and yet he is one of the
seven, and he is going to perdition. The ten horns you 12
saw are ten kings who have not yet begun to reign, but
who for one hour are to share with the beast the exercise
of royal authority; for they have but a single purpose 13
among them and will confer their power and authority
upon the beast. They will wage war upon the Lamb, but 14
the Lamb will defeat them, for he is Lord of lords and
King of kings, and his victory will be shared by his
followers, called and chosen and faithful.'

15   Then he said to me, 'The ocean you saw, where the great whore sat, is an ocean of peoples and populations, 16 nations and languages. As for the ten horns you saw, they together with the beast will come to hate the whore; they will strip her naked and leave her desolate, they will 17 batten on her flesh and burn her to ashes. For God has put it into their heads to carry out his purpose, by making common cause and conferring their sovereignty upon 18 the beast until all that God has spoken is fulfilled. The woman you saw is the great city that holds sway over the kings of the earth.'

✱ 8. Here is a clear example of the belief that Nero would reappear from the underworld: *he who once was alive, and is alive no longer, but has yet to ascend out of the abyss before going to perdition.* The world of men will be *astonished* at his reappearance, *for he once was alive, and is alive no longer, and has still to appear.*

9–10. A double interpretation is given of the seven heads of the monster. In verse 9 they represent *seven hills on which the woman sits.* It was well known that Rome was built on seven hills (the Palatine, Capitoline, Quirinal, Aventine, Esquiline, Viminal and Caelian hills); the author here has forsaken veiled terms and symbols and has given an unmistakable clue that his prophecy is directed against Rome. But in verse 10 the heads are said to correspond also to *seven kings* and what he says of these is of some importance.

10. Is it possible to identify the kings intended by these words: *five have already fallen, one is now reigning, and the other has yet to come*? Since Julius Caesar was not emperor, we should probably begin with Augustus. He was followed by Tiberius, Caligula, Claudius and Nero. These five have died at the time of writing, and the successor of Nero is reigning as number 6. A seventh emperor will follow. At first sight we assume that as Nero's successor was Galba, this particular

passage must have been originally written during his reign, 68–69. The writer expected that another emperor would follow Galba, but the reign of this seventh emperor would be a brief one, and then (as we shall see when we consider verse 11) Nero would return as the Antichrist.

Galba reigned for only about six months; anyone writing during this brief reign would of course be quite unaware that it would end so soon and that two other emperors would be dead before the year was over. The year 69 is known as the year of the four emperors: Galba, Otho, Vitellius and Vespasian. Because of the brevity of the reigns of the first three, many authorities think that they should be dismissed from the reckoning, and that Vespasian (69–79) should be regarded as the true successor of Nero. His ten years' reign would perhaps be a more likely period for the writing of the original oracle taken over here. The Roman historian Suetonius dismisses the three brief reigns in question as virtually equivalent to rebellions. The arguments in support of the view that the final version of Revelation was produced under Domitian (81–96) still remain, and it is not really vital to be able to date with certainty any fragments which may have been incorporated.

There would be nothing unusual in the writer of an apocalypse embodying earlier material and leaving it unchanged; and it would not be difficult for John to give the cryptic terms of this prophecy his own meaning. This adaptation would be easy by counting from Caligula. Augustus and Tiberius were not fanatics in the matter of emperor-worship. It was in Caligula's time that the matter provoked a crisis. He madly planned to erect an image of himself in the temple at Jerusalem but died before this was put into effect. If then we begin the reckoning with him and again ignore the three short reigns as before, the sixth who *is now reigning* is precisely Domitian, the preceding five being Caligula, Claudius, Nero, Vespasian and Titus.

11. It is fairly clear that Nero is intended here. The series

of seven kings will be followed by *an eighth*, identified with *the beast*; but he is in reality *one of the seven* because Nero was widely expected by Jews, Christians and pagans, to reappear. Number 8 does not add a further emperor but is one of the seven appearing again.

12. These *ten kings* should probably be identified with 'the kings from the east' of 16: 12, the Parthians whom popular expectation linked with Nero's reappearance.

14. This verse is sometimes thought to be out of place. But the verb is in the future, *will wage war*; and it may be an anticipatory mention of the battle of 19: 19–21. The beast and his ten allies are destined later to do battle with the Lamb; but at the moment they are concerned with the destruction of Rome (verses 16–18). When this has been accomplished the beast and his allies will presumably sail to Palestine, where the kings of the earth have been building up their armies at Armageddon in preparation for the last great conflict; the beast will place himself at their head (19: 19).

16. *batten*, i.e. feed gluttonously.

burn her to ashes. It is interesting to recall that Nero was suspected of being responsible for the fire of Rome in 64. On his reappearance he is evidently still addicted to arson; this time he is more successful. The words of this verse recall the judgement of the harlot Oholibah (Jerusalem) in Ezek. 23: 25–6: 'thy residue shall be devoured by the fire. They shall also strip thee of thy clothes, and take away thy fair jewels'; cf. Rev. 18: 16. ✶

THE FALL OF BABYLON

18 After this I saw another angel coming down from heaven; he came with great authority and the earth was lit up with
2 his splendour. Then in a mighty voice he proclaimed, 'Fallen, fallen is Babylon the great! She has become a dwelling for demons, a haunt for every unclean spirit,

for every foul and loathsome bird. For all nations 3
have drunk deep of the fierce wine of her fornication;
the kings of the earth have committed fornication with
her, and merchants the world over have grown rich on
her bloated wealth.'

Then I heard another voice from heaven that said: 4
'Come out of her, my people, lest you take part in her
sins and share in her plagues. For her sins are piled high 5
as heaven, and God has not forgotten her crimes. Pay 6
her back in her own coin, repay her twice over for her
deeds! Double for her the strength of the potion she
mixed! Mete out grief and torment to match her 7
voluptuous pomp! She says in her heart, "I am a queen
on my throne! No mourning for me, no widow's
weeds!" Because of this her plagues shall strike her in a 8
single day—pestilence, bereavement, famine, and burning
—for mighty is the Lord God who has pronounced her
doom!'

* This chapter gives a magnificent description of the fall of
Babylon (Rome). The writer's exultation over the burning of
the city is not disguised, for he believed that he was describing
the doom of the great enemy of God's people (verse 20).
There is hardly a phrase which is specifically Christian, apart
from the word *apostles* in verse 20; and it may well be that an
earlier Jewish writing provided the material of this chapter
as of the preceding one. No mention is made of emperor-
worship, so prominent elsewhere in Revelation. Babylon
is condemned for her luxury, uncleanness and corrupting
influence. Added to these is the crime of killing the prophets
and people of God (verse 20). This could well have referred
originally to the frightful massacre of Jews in the disasters of
66–70 when Jerusalem was destroyed. The writer of Revelation

in incorporating this material would of course see new meanings in its words, and would think of Christian martyrdoms under Nero in the 60's and under Domitian in his own period.

The whole chapter is full of Old Testament reminiscences. The description of the fall of Tyre in Ezek. 26–7 is of special importance and should be read in association with the present passage.

1. The splendour of the angel is well conveyed by this touch; the whole earth was lit up by his brightness.

2. Behind this verse lies Isa. 13: 19–22 which told of the old Babylon becoming the lair of doleful creatures, haunted by ostriches and satyrs.

3. For the imagery cf. Isa. 23: 17, 'she [Tyre] shall play the harlot with all the kingdoms of the world upon the face of the earth'.

4. Even this injunction to escape from Babylon in order to avoid sharing in its doom is based upon an Old Testament passage. In Jer. 51: 45 the reference is to ancient Babylon, 'My people, go ye out of the midst of her, and save yourselves every man from the fierce anger of the Lord'.

7. Cf. the boast of Babylon in Isa. 47: 7–8, 'I shall be a lady for ever...I shall not sit as a widow, neither shall I know the loss of children'.

8. The passage just quoted from Isaiah is followed by a prophecy of disaster 'in a moment in one day' (47: 9); so here plagues are to strike the new Babylon *in a single day*. ✳

LAMENT OVER BABYLON—AND EXULTATION

9 The kings of the earth who committed fornication with her and wallowed in her luxury will weep and wail over
10 her, as they see the smoke of her conflagration. They will stand at a distance, for horror at her torment, and will say, 'Alas, alas for the great city, the mighty city of Babylon! In a single hour your doom has struck!'

The merchants of the earth also will weep and mourn 11 for her, because no one any longer buys their cargoes, cargoes of gold and silver, jewels and pearls, cloths of 12 purple and scarlet, silks and fine linens; all kinds of scented woods, ivories, and every sort of thing made of costly woods, bronze, iron, or marble; cinnamon and 13 spice, incense, perfumes and frankincense; wine, oil, flour and wheat, sheep and cattle, horses, chariots, slaves, and the lives of men. 'The fruit you longed for', they 14 will say, 'is gone from you; all the glitter and the glamour are lost, never to be yours again!' The traders in all these 15 wares, who gained their wealth from her, will stand at a distance for horror at her torment, weeping and mourning and saying, 'Alas, alas for the great city, that was clothed 16 in fine linen and purple and scarlet, bedizened with gold and jewels and pearls! Alas that in one hour so much 17 wealth should be laid waste!'

Then all the sea-captains and voyagers, the sailors and those who traded by sea, stood at a distance and cried 18 out as they saw the smoke of her conflagration: 'Was there ever a city like the great city?' They threw dust on 19 their heads, weeping and mourning and saying, 'Alas, alas for the great city, where all who had ships at sea grew rich on her wealth! Alas that in a single hour she should be laid waste!'

But let heaven exult over her; exult, apostles and 20 prophets and people of God; for in the judgement against her he has vindicated your cause!

Then a mighty angel took up a stone like a great mill- 21 stone and hurled it into the sea and said, 'Thus shall Babylon, the great city, be sent hurtling down, never to

22 be seen again! No more shall the sound of harpers and minstrels, of flute-players and trumpeters, be heard in you; no more shall craftsmen of any trade be found in you; no more shall the sound of the mill be heard in you;
23 no more shall the light of the lamp be seen in you; no more shall the voice of the bride and bridegroom be heard in you! Your traders were once the merchant princes of the world, and with your sorcery you deceived all the nations.'

24 For the blood of the prophets and of God's people was found in her, the blood of all who had been done to death on earth.

✶ 9–10. *The kings of the earth* stand at a distance, watching the mighty blaze as Babylon is destroyed and lamenting over her. Cf. Ezek. 26: 16–17, 'Then all the princes of the sea...shall take up a lamentation for thee, and say to thee, How art thou destroyed...the renowned city'.

11. Those who trafficked with Tyre are described in Ezek. 27: 31, 'they shall weep for thee in bitterness of soul with bitter mourning'. Verse 36 of the same chapter refers to *the merchants*.

12–16. Again Ezek. 27 supplies the imagery here; the wares of Tyre are given in detail, 'ivory and ebony (27: 15),... emeralds, purple, and broidered work, and fine linen' (27: 16).

In verses 12–14 the arrangement is mainly in fours, similar commodities being grouped together. The scheme is not carried out completely but the following may be noted: gold and silver, jewels and pearls;—purple and scarlet, silks and fine linens;—costly woods, bronze, iron, marble;—wine, oil, flour and wheat;—sheep and cattle, horses, chariots. *Slaves, and the lives of men* (literally 'souls of men') round off the list; they come last perhaps because they are regarded as of least account.

17-20. Notice the contrast between the lament of the sea-captains and traders and the exultation of *heaven* and the *people of God*. The question, *Was there ever a city like the great city?* resembles Ezek. 27: 32, 'Who is there like Tyre, like her that is brought to silence in the midst of the sea?'

17. In Ezek. 27 the destruction of Tyre is depicted as the ruin of a great ship whose fittings are set out in graphic detail; those who behold this disaster 'stand upon the land' as they watch (27: 29). Here in Revelation the calamity is a burning city, and the spectators stand *at a distance*.

19. Even the gesture of throwing dust on the head comes from Ezek. 27: 30 which follows the verse just quoted, 'and shall cast up dust upon their heads'.

21. The imagery of the *millstone* is taken from Jer. 51: 63-4, where the prophet is told to bind a stone to his scroll and to cast it into the river saying, 'Thus shall Babylon sink, and shall not rise again because of the evil that I will bring upon her'.

22-4. This scene of desolation reminds one of similar features in Jeremiah's pathetic description of devastated Judah, 'I will take from them the voice of mirth and the voice of gladness, the voice of the bridegroom and the voice of the bride, the sound of the millstones, and the light of the candle' (25: 10). *

SONGS OF VICTORY

After this I heard what sounded like the roar of a vast **19** throng in heaven; and they were shouting:

'Alleluia! Victory and glory and power belong to our **2** God, for true and just are his judgements! He has condemned the great whore who corrupted the earth with her fornication, and has avenged upon her the blood of his servants.'

3 Then once more they shouted:

'Alleluia! The smoke goes up from her for ever and ever!'

4 And the twenty-four elders and the four living creatures fell down and worshipped God as he sat on the throne, and they too cried:

'Amen! Alleluia!'

5 Then a voice came from the throne which said:

'Praise our God, all you his servants, you that fear him, both great and small!'

6 Again I heard what sounded like a vast crowd, like the noise of rushing water and deep roars of thunder, and they cried:

'Alleluia! The Lord our God, sovereign over all, has
7 entered on his reign! Exult and shout for joy and do him homage, for the wedding-day of the Lamb has
8 come! His bride has made herself ready, and for her dress she has been given fine linen, clean and shining.'

(Now the fine linen signifies the righteous deeds of God's people.)

9 Then the angel said to me, 'Write this: "Happy are those who are invited to the wedding-supper of the Lamb!"' And he added, 'These are the very words of
10 God.' At this I fell at his feet to worship him. But he said to me, 'No, not that! I am but a fellow-servant with you and your brothers who bear their testimony to Jesus. It is God you must worship. Those who bear testimony to Jesus are inspired like the prophets.'

✻ This chapter is in two main parts. 1–10 presents the triumphant shout of victory in heaven at the fall of Babylon, and also hints at the preparations for the wedding of the Lamb and his bride. 11–21 describes the return of Christ and the destruction of his foes.

1. In the previous chapter it was said, 'let heaven exult over her' (18: 20). Now we hear heaven exulting. This section provides another example of the alternating of judgements on earth and songs of worship in heaven.

2. *Alleluia!* This word, familiar to us from hymns, is found several times in the book of Psalms, but in the New Testament it occurs only in this passage, verses 1–6. It is the transliteration of the Hebrew for 'Praise God'.

3–8. The second shout of the *vast throng* is followed by the cry of the elders and the living creatures (verse 4), a voice from the throne (verse 5) and the shout of the vast crowd again (verses 6–8). These cries of *Alleluia* inevitably remind us of the Hallelujah Chorus in Handel's *Messiah*; the words of this famous chorus are taken partly from this chapter and partly from Rev. 11: 15.

7. In the Old Testament Israel is at times regarded as the consort of God and in the New Testament the same idea is applied to the Church, the new Israel, here named the Lamb's *bride*. See Eph. 5: 25–33; and 2 Cor. 11: 2, 'I betrothed you to Christ, thinking to present you as a chaste virgin to her true and only husband'.

9. The actual *wedding-supper of the Lamb* is nowhere described.

10. This mistaken attempt to worship an angel is repeated in 22: 8–9. Cornelius' prostration before Peter, in Acts 10: 25–6, is somewhat similar. There is evidence that in certain Jewish circles at this period there was a practice of angel-worship; it appears to be referred to also in Col. 2: 18, 'people who go in for self-mortification and angel-worship'.

The closing sentence of this verse may be interpreted in different ways, and the alternative translation in the N.E.B.

footnote gives the rendering, 'For testimony to Jesus is the spirit that inspires prophets'. The point seems to be that the angel and prophets like John were alike concerned with *testimony to Jesus*. They did not draw attention to themselves, and so any kind of honour or worship (such as John had offered to the angel) was inappropriate. *It is God you must worship.* ✳

THE RETURN OF CHRIST

11 Then I saw heaven wide open, and there before me was a white horse; and its rider's name was Faithful and True,
12 for he is just in judgement and just in war. His eyes flamed like fire, and on his head were many diadems. Written upon him was a name known to none but
13 himself, and he was robed in a garment drenched in
14 blood. He was called the Word of God, and the armies of heaven followed him on white horses, clothed in fine
15 linen, clean and shining. From his mouth there went a sharp sword with which to smite the nations; for he it is who shall rule them with an iron rod, and tread the wine-press of the wrath and retribution of God the sovereign
16 Lord. And on his robe and on his leg there was written the name: 'King of kings and Lord of lords.'

17   Then I saw an angel standing in the sun, and he cried aloud to all the birds flying in mid-heaven: 'Come and
18 gather for God's great supper, to eat the flesh of kings and commanders and fighting men, the flesh of horses and their riders, the flesh of all men, slave and free, great
19 and small!' Then I saw the beast and the kings of the earth and their armies mustered to do battle with the
20 Rider and his army. The beast was taken prisoner, and so was the false prophet who had worked miracles in its

presence and deluded those that had received the mark of
the beast and worshipped its image. The two of them
were thrown alive into the lake of fire with its sulphurous
flames. The rest were killed by the sword which went 21
out of the Rider's mouth; and all the birds gorged themselves on their flesh.

✻ 11–16. This is one of the most detailed and vivid presenta-
tions of the return of Christ to be found in the New Testament;
cf. 1 Thess. 4: 16–18. He is described as descending from
heaven to earth on a white horse and followed by angelic
armies mounted in a similar way.

13. The *garment drenched in blood* is a reminiscence of
Isa. 63: 1–6, a passage which in a pictorial fashion shows God
taking vengeance upon Edom. The New Testament often
applies to Jesus passages originally written about God, and
this is the case here. Isa. 63: 2 asks the question, 'Wherefore
art thou red in thine apparel...?' And the answer includes
the words, 'I trod them [i.e. the peoples] in mine anger, and
trampled them in my fury; and their lifeblood is sprinkled
upon my garments'. Elsewhere in Revelation, and in the New
Testament generally, Christ sheds his own blood for others;
here alone is he stained with the blood of his foes.

14. *He was called the Word of God.* This is a remarkable link
with the Prologue of John's Gospel (1: 1–18) where the pre-
existent Son of God is called the Word. Here is one of several
points of contact between the Gospel and Revelation. Though
the basic attitudes of the two writings are very different, there
are certain expressions which were apparently current in
Asia, the area from which all the Johannine works probably
came. The description of Jesus as a Lamb is a similar instance,
though the Greek word is different (John 1: 29, 36).

15. The sword coming from his mouth has some connexion
with Isa. 11: 4; and 49: 2, 'he hath made my mouth like a
sharp sword'.

16. *on his leg*. Literally 'thigh'. The name was perhaps written upon a fold of the dress which fell across the thigh.

17–21. The beast and his allies are defeated. Their armies are slain and birds of prey are summoned to gorge themselves on their flesh (cf. Ezek. 39: 17). This is *God's great supper* (verse 17), a grim counterpart of *the wedding-supper of the Lamb* (verse 9).

19. *to do battle*. The final battle now takes place; it is first mentioned in anticipation in 16: 14–16 where all the kings of the world begin to muster at Armageddon for 'the great day of battle of God the sovereign Lord'. As we saw earlier, these *kings of the earth* should be distinguished from 'the kings from the east' (16: 12); the latter are to be identified with those who supported the beast's attack on Rome (17: 12–13). Now the battle is on a much bigger scale; it is the final world-conflict in which all *the kings of the earth* take part.

20. The beast and the false prophet are cast alive into hell, *the lake of fire* (see 20: 14 note). For the fate of the devil, the prime mover behind all these evil forces, we must turn to the beginning of the next chapter. *

THE MILLENNIUM

20 Then I saw an angel coming down from heaven with the
2 key of the abyss and a great chain in his hands. He seized the dragon, that serpent of old, the Devil or Satan, and
3 chained him up for a thousand years; he threw him into the abyss, shutting and sealing it over him, so that he might seduce the nations no more till the thousand years were over. After that he must be let loose for a short while.

4 Then I saw thrones, and upon them sat those to whom judgement was committed. I could see the souls of those who had been beheaded for the sake of God's word and their testimony to Jesus, those who had not worshipped

the beast and its image or received its mark on forehead
or hand. These came to life again and reigned with Christ
for a thousand years, though the rest of the dead did not 5
come to life until the thousand years were over. This
is the first resurrection. Happy indeed, and one of God's 6
own people, is the man who shares in this first resurrection! Upon such the second death has no claim; but they
shall be priests of God and of Christ, and shall reign with
him for the thousand years.

When the thousand years are over, Satan will be let 7
loose from his dungeon; and he will come out to seduce 8
the nations in the four quarters of the earth and to muster
them for battle, yes, the hosts of Gog and Magog,
countless as the sands of the sea. So they marched over 9
the breadth of the land and laid siege to the camp of
God's people and the city that he loves. But fire came
down on them from heaven and consumed them; and the 10
Devil, their seducer, was flung into the lake of fire and
sulphur, where the beast and the false prophet had been
flung, there to be tormented day and night for ever.

* The thousand years reign, the main theme of this section,
is known as the Millennium, a Latin word meaning a period
of this length (from *mille*, thousand, and *annus*, year). It is one
of the most remarkable features of Revelation. Those martyred
in the great persecution are to be raised from the dead to
share in the reign of Christ, who is regarded as personally
present on earth following his return (19: 11-16). To understand this it is necessary to bear in mind the Jewish expectations
concerning the Messiah. The Jews, or many of them, thought
that when the Messiah came he would reign for a limited
period; this is what orthodox Jews believe today. In the
apocalypses and other Jewish writings various periods are

suggested for the length of this reign, 400 years, 40, 1000. At the end of it there would be the resurrection of the dead and after that the new heaven and earth, which would last for ever. This is the scheme which Revelation follows. The martyrs alone rise at the beginning of the thousand years; *the rest of the dead* (verse 5) are raised at the end of it (verses 12–13). The new heaven and earth follow in 21: 1.

1–2. Satan is chained for the period of Christ's reign on earth. The same four titles are given as in 12: 9 (*dragon*, etc.).

3. The release of Satan for a short time is a point taken up in verses 7–10.

5–6. *The first resurrection* is for those *beheaded* (verse 4) in the course of *the beast's* onslaught. They now reign with their Lord. *The second death* is defined in verse 14; see 2: 11 and note.

7. It is difficult to see what purpose is served by this temporary release of Satan, after he has been securely imprisoned. There are mythological parallels. The Babylonian legend of Tiamat (see 12: 3 note) said that this chaos-monster would be released at the end of history and would again be defeated by Marduk. Thus the end of time would resemble the beginning—an important principle of apocalyptic thought.

8. *the hosts of Gog and Magog.* Ezek. 38–9 describes the invasion of the hosts of 'Gog, of the land of Magog, the prince of Rosh, Meshech, and Tubal'; with them nations from every quarter gather in a final assault against God's people. Similarly here *nations in the four quarters of the earth* (apparently identified with *the hosts of Gog and Magog*) are mustered against the holy city. This fresh outburst of evil is explained by the release of Satan who seduces the nations and incites them to rebel at the end of the Millennium (verse 7).

In Ezekiel Gog's incursion of 38–9 follows the chapters devoted to the Messianic kingdom (33–7) and this may explain its position here. Moreover the invasion provided an opportunity for including a final siege of Jerusalem (Zech. 14) which John had not allowed for earlier; now the traditional attack on *the camp of God's people and the city that he loves* (verse 9) finds a place.

9-10. The revolt is to be of short duration; and with the final suppression of the devil the way is open for an entirely righteous and blissful future. But first there must be the general resurrection and the final judgement (verses 11-15). *

THE LAST JUDGEMENT

Then I saw a great white throne, and the One who sat 11 upon it; from his presence earth and heaven vanished away, and no place was left for them. I could see the 12 dead, great and small, standing before the throne; and books were opened. Then another book was opened, the roll of the living. From what was written in these books the dead were judged upon the record of their deeds. The sea gave up its dead, and Death and Hades 13 gave up the dead in their keeping; they were judged, each man on the record of his deeds. Then Death and 14 Hades were flung into the lake of fire. This lake of fire is the second death; and into it were flung any whose names 15 were not to be found in the roll of the living.

* This is one of the most impressive descriptions of the Last Judgement ever written, in spite of its brevity. It is a mistake to interpret every detail of this 'great assize' in a literal fashion; but the fact of judgement and of man's responsibility to God remains. Paul is more reticent than the apocalyptist and is content to say, 'For we must all have our lives laid open before the tribunal of Christ' (2 Cor. 5: 10).

11. The judge is apparently God the Father. In the judgement of Matt. 25: 31-46 this place is taken by 'the Son of Man'.

12. *and books were opened*, as in the judgement scene of Dan. 7: 10.

13. *The sea gave up its dead.* This is connected with the resurrection and refers to those who had lost their lives by drowning.

14. *Death and Hades* are destroyed after giving up *the dead in their keeping* (verse 13). They almost appear to be personified. But the point is that there is no longer any place for them. Hades was the temporary abode of the dead, not their final destination; it has no further use. And Death is also brought to an end (21: 4).

lake of fire. The fire awaiting men after death had at one time been thought of as a purifying fire; but later it came to be regarded as a means of punishment or destruction. In some passages of the New Testament the thought of purifying fire may be present. But in Revelation it is clearly regarded as a form of everlasting punishment. ✳

THE NEW HEAVEN AND EARTH

21 Then I saw a new heaven and a new earth, for the first heaven and the first earth had vanished, and there was no
2 longer any sea. I saw the holy city, new Jerusalem, coming down out of heaven from God, made ready like
3 a bride adorned for her husband. I heard a loud voice proclaiming from the throne: 'Now at last God has his dwelling among men! He will dwell among them and they shall be his people, and God himself will be with
4 them. He will wipe every tear from their eyes; there shall be an end to death, and to mourning and crying and pain; for the old order has passed away!'

5   Then he who sat on the throne said, 'Behold! I am making all things new!' And he said to me, 'Write this
6 down; for these words are trustworthy and true. Indeed',

he said, 'they are already fulfilled. For I am the Alpha
and the Omega, the beginning and the end. A draught
from the water-springs of life will be my free gift to the
thirsty. All this is the victor's heritage; and I will be his 7
God and he shall be my son. But as for the cowardly, 8
the faithless, and the vile, murderers, fornicators, sorcerers,
idolaters, and liars of every kind, their lot will be the
second death, in the lake that burns with sulphurous
flames.'

✻ After the Last Judgement comes a description of the
eternal blessedness of the saints. 'From the smoke and pain
and heat of the preceding scenes it is a relief to pass into the
clear, clean atmosphere of the eternal morning where the
breath of heaven is sweet and the vast city of God sparkles like
a diamond in the radiance of his presence' (J. Moffatt,
Expositor's Greek Testament).

1. *a new heaven and a new earth*. Similar language is found
in Isa. 65: 17, which is no doubt the source of the present
reference. Study of this idea in the apocalypses and elsewhere
shows that what was expected was not the annihilation of the
present universe, but rather its cleansing, renewal and
restoration, so that it would seem to be a new creation.

We take it for granted today that the people of God will
spend eternity in heaven. But here there is something quite
different—a new heaven and earth, and the saints are to live
upon the renewed earth. The new Jerusalem comes *down out
of heaven from God* (verses 2 and 10).

there was no longer any sea. Behind this strange announcement lies the fact that the Jews regarded the sea as a hostile
force which God had to tame and control. This goes back
ultimately to the Babylonian legend of Tiamat, the sea-
monster who was imprisoned in its depths (Amos 9: 3).

2. *the holy city* is seen descending again in verse 10. How
are we to account for this? It may be that in verse 2 John sees

it beginning a long slow descent from heaven and setting out
on its journey, while in verse 10 its descent is nearly completed.
Verses 1-5 are introductory and look forward; everything
is in a summary form. In verse 10, however, a more extended
description begins. New Jerusalem is now ending its descent
and taking its position on the new earth; and as it lies secure
and square its radiant qualities are passed under review.

3. This is the fulfilment of God's age-long purpose. In a
sense it is a theme that runs through the Bible. In the beginning
communion between man and God was lost and man hid
from God (Gen. 3: 8). But God asked, 'Where art thou?'
(3: 9) and through the ages he has been seeking his lost
children and endeavouring in one way and another, supremely
in Jesus Christ, to repair the broken relationship.

4. Another saying from Isaiah finds here its perfect setting:
'the Lord God will wipe away tears from off all faces' (25: 8).

5. Apart from 1: 8 this is the only time in Revelation that
God speaks.

8. *the cowardly* are put in the forefront of the black list. In
the days of persecution great courage was needed, especially in
the matter of emperor-worship. ✳

THE NEW JERUSALEM

9 Then one of the seven angels that held the seven bowls
full of the seven last plagues came and spoke to me and
said, 'Come, and I will show you the bride, the wife of the
10 Lamb.' So in the Spirit he carried me away to a great
high mountain, and showed me the holy city of Jerusalem
11 coming down out of heaven from God. It shone with the
glory of God; it had the radiance of some priceless jewel,
12 like a jasper, clear as crystal. It had a great high wall,
with twelve gates, at which were twelve angels; and on
the gates were inscribed the names of the twelve tribes

of Israel. There were three gates to the east, three to the 13
north, three to the south, and three to the west. The 14
city wall had twelve foundation-stones, and on them were
the names of the twelve apostles of the Lamb.

The angel who spoke with me carried a gold measur- 15
ing-rod, to measure the city, its wall, and its gates. The 16
city was built as a square, and was as wide as it was long.
It measured by his rod twelve thousand furlongs, its
length and breadth and height being equal. Its wall was 17
one hundred and forty-four cubits high, that is, by human
measurements, which the angel was using. The wall was 18
built of jasper, while the city itself was of pure gold,
bright as clear glass. The foundations of the city wall were 19
adorned with jewels of every kind, the first of the
foundation-stones being jasper, the second lapis lazuli,
the third chalcedony, the fourth emerald, the fifth 20
sardonyx, the sixth cornelian, the seventh chrysolite, the
eighth beryl, the ninth topaz, the tenth chrysoprase, the
eleventh turquoise, and the twelfth amethyst. The twelve 21
gates were twelve pearls, each gate being made from a
single pearl. The streets of the city were of pure gold,
like translucent glass.

* The description of *the holy city* (the wife of the Lamb) is in
marked contrast to that of the city of Babylon (the whore) in
chapter 18.

10. In Ezek. 40: 2 at the beginning of his description of the
holy city there are similar words, 'In the visions of God
brought he me into the land of Israel, and set me down upon
a very high mountain, whereon was as it were the frame of a
city [i.e. a structure like a city] on the south'.

12. *on the gates...the names of the twelve tribes of Israel*;
and on the *foundation-stones...the names of the twelve apostles*

(verse 14). These two series of twelve set forth the complete harmony between the old covenant and the new.

14. Cf. Eph. 2: 20, 'built upon the foundation of the apostles and prophets' (as in the N.E.B. footnote).

16. *its length and breadth and height being equal.* A city shaped like a cube is difficult to conceive, but the point may be that it corresponds to the cube-shaped Holy of Holies in the temple. According to verse 22 there is to be no temple in the city. All the inhabitants have free access to God. Under the Jewish regime only the high priest could enter the Holy of Holies, and that only once a year; but Christ has destroyed the veil of separation which kept men out and has opened a new and living way by which all are invited to approach. This is one of the main themes of Hebrews and it may be that a similar thought finds pictorial expression here. The city is of vast dimensions, about 1500 miles each way.

18–20. The main thought comes from Isa. 54: 11–12 where God says to Israel, 'I will set thy stones in fair colours, and lay thy foundations with sapphires. And I will make thy pinnacles of rubies, and thy gates of carbuncles, and all thy border of pleasant stones.' In amplifying this thought and applying it to the twelve-fold scheme of the city John turns to the twelve gems on the breastplate of the high priest (Exod. 28: 15–21) on which were engraved the names of the tribes of Israel. (There are some differences in the naming of the jewels in the two lists, and the exact meaning of their names is not certain in every case.) The twelve jewels worn by the high priest alone are now the very foundation of the city. The city itself is as sacred as the Holy of Holies and all the inhabitants are 'named the priests of the Lord' (Isa. 61: 6); cf. Rev. 1: 6.

21. John Bunyan in his commentary on this chapter (*The New Jerusalem*) suggested that the paving *of pure gold* derived from the temple, whose floor was overlaid with gold (1 Kings 6: 30). If this is correct it is another example of the tendency just noted. ✻

A CITY OF LIGHT AND LIVING WATER

I saw no temple in the city; for its temple was the 22
sovereign Lord God and the Lamb. And the city had no 23
need of sun or moon to shine upon it; for the glory of
God gave it light, and its lamp was the Lamb. By its 24
light shall the nations walk, and the kings of the earth
shall bring into it all their splendour. The gates of the 25
city shall never be shut by day—and there will be no
night. The wealth and splendour of the nations shall be 26
brought into it; but nothing unclean shall enter, nor 27
anyone whose ways are false or foul, but only those who
are inscribed in the Lamb's roll of the living.

Then he showed me the river of the water of life, **22**
sparkling like crystal, flowing from the throne of God
and of the Lamb down the middle of the city's street. 2
On either side of the river stood a tree of life, which
yields twelve crops of fruit, one for each month of the
year. The leaves of the trees serve for the healing of the
nations, and every accursed thing shall disappear. The 3
throne of God and of the Lamb will be there, and his
servants shall worship him; they shall see him face to 4
face, and bear his name on their foreheads. There shall 5
be no more night, nor will they need the light of lamp or
sun, for the Lord God will give them light; and they
shall reign for evermore.

✻ Two factors which the Jews associated with the future age
were abundance of light and water; they are both mentioned
in Zech. 14: 7–8. Both are prominent in this section.

22. *I saw no temple in the city*. This is in marked contrast to
the prophecy of Ezekiel. We have seen throughout that John

is strongly influenced by the language and ideas and even the outline of Ezekiel. Yet at this point there is a significant divergence. Ezekiel spends four long chapters (40–3) in a detailed description of the new temple. But, says John, *I saw no temple in the city*. The city itself is shaped like the Holy of Holies; the immediate presence of God is no longer in a reserved place solemnly marked off, but he is accessible to all. The redeemed are a kingdom of priests and all share in the light of God's presence. 'In that day shall there be upon the bells of the horses, HOLY UNTO THE LORD.... Yea, every pot in Jerusalem and in Judah shall be holy unto the LORD of hosts' (Zech. 14: 20–1).

its temple was the sovereign Lord God and the Lamb. Cf. Ezek. 11: 16, 'yet will I be to them a sanctuary'.

23. Behind this lies Isa. 60: 19, 'The sun shall be no more thy light by day; neither for brightness shall the moon give light unto thee: but the Lord shall be unto thee an everlasting light, and thy God thy glory'.

24. The same chapter of Isaiah gives the basic idea again, 'And nations shall come to thy light' (60: 3); and again in the same chapter, 'the wealth of the nations shall come unto thee' (60: 5). The new Jerusalem is the centre of the new earth but not its sole place of residence. But in the case of these Old Testament quotations and echoes it is a mistake to press the full force of every word. The prophets were thinking mainly of a future under the historical conditions of our present life. John makes use of their sublime visions, lifting them on to the eternal plane; and at times he retains words not entirely appropriate to this new setting.

25. *The gates of the city shall never be shut.* Cf. Isa. 60: 11, 'Thy gates also shall be open continually'.

27. Nothing unclean is to sully the purity of the city, just as 'the holy city' of Isa. 52: 1 was to be barred to 'the unclean'.

22: 1. The description of the river of life is reminiscent of Ezek. 47: 1–12 which gives a memorable picture of the waters issuing from under the threshold of the house. Though Ezekiel does not call his stream a river of life, he does say, 'every thing shall live whithersoever the river cometh' (47: 9). Ezekiel's river proceeds from the temple described so fully in chapters 40–3; but in John's city there is no temple, its place being taken by the *Lord God and the Lamb* (21: 22). Accordingly the river comes from *the throne of God and of the Lamb*.

2. Ezekiel's river had trees beside it (47: 7) and their leaves were for *healing* (47: 12). Similar ideas are repeated here. But the picture is enriched by the memory of Gen. 2, with its *tree of life* in the garden of Eden.

the healing of the nations. After the bitter annals of human history mankind finds peace and restoration.

3. *every accursed thing*. This perhaps looks back to Gen. 3: 17–18. After the Fall, man was debarred from the garden with the tree of life and a curse was imposed; thorns and thistles began to grow. Now the way of access to the tree is open (verses 14 and 19) and the curse is taken away. Thus the last chapters of the Bible balance the first, and Paradise Lost gives place to Paradise Regained.

his servants shall worship him. This could be linked with the *name on their foreheads* (verse 4); the high priest in Exod. 28: 36–8 had the words 'Holy to the Lord' on his forehead. Now the whole community offers priestly worship.

4. *they shall see him face to face*. Cf. 1 Cor. 13: 12, 'Now we see only puzzling reflections in a mirror, but then we shall see face to face'. These closing verses (3–5) give a wonderful description of the eternal life: perfect communion, worship, the vision of God, light and victory.

his name. This may imply a new name hinted at in 19: 12; 3: 12. In the Bible, names are of great importance; and the word occurs nearly 40 times in Revelation. Each great era is associated with some new name of God: (*a*) to the patriarchs he was the Almighty (see Exod. 6: 3); (*b*) Israel knew him as Yahweh; (*c*) Jesus brought a new name of God; 'I made thy name known to them' (John 17: 26); (*d*) it is not surprising that the future age will bring a name as yet unknown, some further disclosure from the depths of the divine nature.

5. This emphasis on perpetual light is a repetition of 21: 23–5 but it provides a fitting close to the description of eternal blessedness with which the main part of the book now closes. The remainder of the chapter consists of short sayings and closing exhortations. ✻

CLOSING WARNINGS AND PROMISES

6 Then he said to me, 'These words are trustworthy and true. The Lord God who inspires the prophets has sent his angel to show his servants what must shortly happen.
7 And, remember, I am coming soon!'

Happy is the man who heeds the words of prophecy
8 contained in this book! It is I, John, who heard and saw these things. And when I had heard and seen them, I fell in worship at the feet of the angel who had shown them
9 to me. But he said to me, 'No, not that! I am but a fellow-servant with you and your brothers the prophets and those who heed the words of this book. It is God
10 you must worship.' Then he told me, 'Do not seal up the words of prophecy in this book, for the hour of
11 fulfilment is near. Meanwhile, let the evil-doer go on doing evil and the filthy-minded wallow in his filth, but let the good man persevere in his goodness and the dedicated man be true to his dedication.'

12 'Yes, I am coming soon, and bringing my recompense
13 with me, to requite everyone according to his deeds! I am the Alpha and the Omega, the first and the last, the beginning and the end.'

14 Happy are those who wash their robes clean! They

will have the right to the tree of life and will enter by
the gates of the city. Outside are dogs, sorcerers and 15
fornicators, murderers and idolaters, and all who love
and practise deceit.

'I, Jesus, have sent my angel to you with this testimony 16
for the churches. I am the root and scion of David, the
bright morning star.'

'Come!' say the Spirit and the bride. 17

'Come!' let each hearer reply.

Come forward, you who are thirsty; accept the water
of life, a free gift to all who desire it.

For my part, I give this warning to everyone who is 18
listening to the words of prophecy in this book: should
anyone add to them, God will add to him the plagues
described in this book; should anyone take away from 19
the words in this book of prophecy, God will take away
from him his share in the tree of life and the Holy City,
described in this book.

He who gives this testimony speaks: 'Yes, I am coming 20
soon!'

Amen. Come, Lord Jesus!

The grace of the Lord Jesus be with you all. 21

∗ 7. To heed the words of the book would mean primarily
to stand fast in the great persecution so soon to burst upon the
Church.

8. *It is I, John.* Elsewhere he names himself only in 1: 1, 4,
9. The mistaken attempt to worship the angel occurs also in
19: 10.

10. This is in marked contrast to the command given to
Daniel in Dan. 8: 26 and 12: 4, 9. Daniel is supposed to be
writing in the sixth century but his prophecy refers to the
second. Accordingly 'the words are shut up and sealed till

the time of the end' (12: 9). But in the case of Revelation the fulfilment is expected immediately; and so he is told *not to seal up the words of prophecy in this book, for the hour of fulfilment is near.*

11. John's prophecy related to the immediate future and there was no time now for 'many' to 'purify themselves' (as in Dan. 12: 9); instead, the wicked man may as well remain in his wickedness and the good man continue in his goodness, for the judge was at hand with his *recompense* (verse 12).

13. *the Alpha and the Omega.* See 1: 8 and note.

14. The washing of one's robes is in 7: 14 connected with the sacrifice of Christ; it is not a matter of self-reformation but the saving and purifying effect of the cross of Christ.

15. *Outside* does not mean they are in close proximity to the city; for the idea, compare the outer darkness in Matt. 8: 12.

16. *I, Jesus.* This is explained by the words at the opening, 1: 1-2. There is mention of the *angel* also in 1: 1. For *the root* of David see 5: 5.

scion: i.e. descendant. The *morning star* is the reward of the victor in 2: 28. Here it is identified with Jesus, and there may be a reference to Num. 24: 17, a passage which the early Christians often connected with him, 'there shall come forth a star out of Jacob'.

17. In view of verse 20 (*Come, Lord Jesus!*) it would be natural to take the double *Come!* here as addressed to him. His answer is given in the words, *Yes, I am coming soon!* (verse 20).

the Spirit apparently means the Spirit who speaks through the prophet John; *the bride* is of course the whole Christian community. The *hearer* would refer to the members of the congregation who listen to the reading of the book (cf. 1: 3). They are bidden to repeat the cry, *Come!* Those listeners who are not yet church members but inquirers are finally invited to come and *accept the water of life*.

18-19. There may be a reminiscence here of Deut. 4: 2, 'Ye

shall not add unto the word which I command you, neither shall ye diminish from it'.

21. A brief benediction brings the book to a close.

BOOKS FOR FURTHER READING

M. Kiddle, *Revelation* (in the Moffatt New Testament Commentary); W. Barclay, *Letters to the Seven Churches* (S.C.M.); Austin Farrer, *The Revelation of St John the Divine* (Oxford, Clarendon Press). Two older works are still of value: C. Anderson Scott, *Revelation* (in the Century Bible), and A. S. Peake, *The Revelation of John*, which is not a commentary but gives an admirable exposition of the book chapter by chapter. For those who know Greek, the fullest work is R. H. Charles, *Revelation*, 2 vols. (in the International Critical Commentary); readers who know no Greek may nevertheless consult this with profit. The marginal references in the Revised Version of the Bible should not be neglected; these are often as enlightening as any commentary. *

* * * * * * * * * * * * *

INDEX

The references are to pages

INDEX